4/14
Y
B
HOL

1 Year, **100** Pounds

My Journey to a Better, Happier Life

Whitney
Holcombe

SIMON PULSE
New York London Toronto Sydney New Delhi

BEYOND WORDS
Hillsboro, Oregon

An imprint of Simon & Schuster
Children's Publishing Division
1230 Avenue of the Americas
New York, NY 10020

20827 N.W. Cornell Road, Suite 500
Hillsboro, Oregon 97124-9808
503-531-8700 / 503-531-8773 fax
www.beyondword.com

This Beyond Words/Simon Pulse edition January 2014

Interior design: Sara E. Blum
Cover design: Karina Granda, Sara E. Blum
The text of this book was set in Adobe Caslon Pro and Avenir.

Manufactured in the United States of America

10 9 8 7 6 5 4 3 2 1

Library of Congress Cataloging-in-Publication Data

Holcombe, Whitney.
1 year, 100 pounds : my journey to a better, happier life / Whitney Holcombe.
pages cm
Audience: 12+
Audience: Grade 7+
Includes bibliographical references.
1. Holcombe, Whitney—Anecdotes. 2. Reducing diets—Anecdotes. 3. Weight loss
Anecdotes. 4. Reducing exercises—Anecdotes. 5. Teenagers—Nutrition—Anecdotes.
I. Title. II. Title: One year, one hundred pounds. III. Title: My journey to a better, happier life.
RM222.2.H5766 2014
613.2'5—dc23

2013014351

ISBN 978-1-58270-408-1 (pbk)
ISBN 978-1-58270-409-8 (hc)
ISBN 978-1-4424-7662-2 (eBook)

Contents

To all of the young girls
struggling to find peace
with their bodies

Foreword

Whitney Holcombe simply gets "it," and in this thoughtful and moving book, she will give "it" to you. This amazing young woman spent her early life suffering from the burdens of being extremely overweight and finally decided to take a walk. That walk changed her life, and her story may well change *your* life.

As a robotic weight-loss surgeon having worked with more than four thousand patients suffering from all types of weight problems and the consequences thereof, I am keenly aware of all of the nitty-gritty details essential to making the weight-loss equation come out favorably. Whitney not only captures these details and expertly delivers them to you; she has successfully lived them, and, in the process, transformed her world. Learning each step on her own, demonstrating tremendous drive and motivation, and without surgery, she found a way to lose 100 pounds in one year, and keep them off. These pages illustrate her incredible journey from severe obesity to a healthy body and a healthy life. As you will read, this journey is not a simple one and it is not a short one, but it is a journey well worth the energy and time to complete. While I perform weight-loss surgery on many who are severely overweight, I teach my patients that weight-loss surgery is only one of many tools in the arsenal of weight-loss weapons. Without adopting a healthy lifestyle—a lifestyle outlined by Whitney in this book—nothing, not even surgery, is effective.

In fact, an overall healthy lifestyle is the inevitable outcome of Whitney's transformed life, and she does amazing work in explaining every essential component of the means to achieve it. This book is definitely a great weight-loss resource; however, it goes far beyond that. The chapters on motivation, setting goals, developing habits, and learning to exercise all come together in a perfect fashion to give you not only the tools for weight-loss success but the tools for success in life.

Whitney suffered all the typical bias and prejudice that, sadly, our society directs toward those who are significantly overweight, leaving her feeling alone and depressed. Yet she survived and then found a way to thrive. She had a vision of the life she wanted to live, and by reading these words, you, too, will find the courage and the motivation to live the life you want to live. Whitney takes what for many overweight people is an unreachable fantasy and makes it a reality. She never loses sight of the need to eat healthy in order to be healthy. Without question, she also gets the exercise component of weight-loss success exactly right, something almost no other diet book accomplishes.

For the young people who will surely enjoy this book, remember that you have an advantage over many somewhat older overweight individuals: you are young! The ravaging of your body by all of the extra pounds has been minimal, and although it is often challenging, you can still exercise at an aggressive enough pace to have significant impact on your weight.

Sprinkled throughout the text are many fantastic life lessons about personal choices and the consequences of them. From what you eat to how many hours you watch TV or play video games, you own the choices, and you own the results. You know the drill: pizza at the sleepover, cupcakes after the soccer game, a friend's birthday party with cake and ice cream. All of those calories add up more quickly than you can imagine. It is mind numbing, and our on-the-go lifestyle itself frequently leads to repeated sugar poisoning and endless hunger.

With particular emphasis, Whitney sheds light on a common problem facing many adolescents and children: eating what their parents and their parents before them routinely ate. I see it every day in my practice: "I always thought that starch was supposed to be part of every meal." This is simply not the case, and one of the many gems to be uncovered in Whitney's story is the nutritional education that she keenly provides for adolescents and their parents alike.

This is a story of making dreams come true through personal choice, motivation, and hard work. Whitney is to be commended and admired not only for her marvelous personal weight-loss success but for capturing her story in these pages and giving help and hope to all who want a healthy life.

—Joseph J. Colella, MD, FACS

Introduction: Moment of Change

By changing nothing, nothing changes.

—*Tony Robbins*

When I was fourteen, I stepped on my bathroom scale and the number 230 glared up at me. That number controlled my life. It was the main source of my unhappiness and the reason I hated who I was. But that was nine years ago and, believe me, much has changed since then. The turning point came one hot, humid August afternoon in northern Virginia.

I was sprawled on the couch in my apartment, the AC rumbling full blast. *Three more weeks before school starts,* I was thinking glumly, *only three more weeks left!* I had started the summer with good intentions. Yep, I was going to exercise every day all summer long so that when I started the ninth grade, my body would be transformed. On the first day of high school I was going to be a knockout. No more "fat girl" jokes, ever!

High school was going to be my new beginning. For once I was going to fit in and feel pretty. Boys were finally going to notice me. I would even get my first boyfriend! My social life would be crowded with new friends and high school parties. Oh, yes, life would be good once I lost the weight—that was the plan. But, at least in my life up until then, things rarely went as planned. Instead of running marathons, I'd lounged around, stuffing myself with junk food. Pizza for breakfast and lunch. Potato chips, burgers, and ice cream for dinner. And brownies for midnight snacks. Oh, and daily exercise? How about speed walking from the fridge to the couch, where I loafed for hours every day watching music videos? Basically, I was doing anything and everything that was *not* going to turn me into a knockout.

Now, at the end of the summer, waves of frustration swept over me as I reflected on how I had wasted my time. Three months! I had had nearly three months to get in shape, but here I was, no closer to my goal than when school had ended. Ugh!!! Why hadn't I gotten off my big butt and just gone for that run?

Once I asked myself the question, I knew the answer. I was afraid. I had never seriously attempted to lose weight before. What if I couldn't do it? What if it was too hard? I mean, 100 pounds! How long would that even take?

For my entire life I had been the shy fat girl, either pitied or teased. I had never been seen as anything more. Everyone who knew me expected me to stay that way. On the rare occasion I told someone about my desire to lead an adventurous life, my words would be only halfheartedly acknowledged. And when I made the announcement to my family that I was going to lose weight, I was met with polite—but not quite sincere—encouragement.

My parents both nodded and gave me a courteous smile, along with a "That's great, honey! Good for you!" But I could tell they didn't quite take me seriously. Their reaction made me feel like I was a seven-year-old child who had just announced she wanted to be Cinderella when she grew up. I don't think my parents or anyone else ever truly expected me to live up to my goals. I guess I sort of never expected to either. How could I honestly believe that one day I would wake up and not be, well, fat? It just seemed impossible! And yet I knew if I was ever going to be happy, I would have to lose the weight.

Such were the thoughts that blazed through my head that afternoon. Second after second, minute after minute, my mind focused on the one truth I had known all along: this was not how I wanted to live. From a young age I had dreamed of a different life, a different me. I so desperately wanted to live that dream . . . and why shouldn't I? Why was I allowing my insecurities to hold me back? Why?

Right then I knew what had to change. I stood up, determination pulsing through every inch of my body. "Mom," I called out, "I'm going for a walk!"

1

My Story

It doesn't matter where you are; you are nowhere compared to where you can go.

—*Bob Proctor*

From the first grade I was known as the "fat girl"—the only fat girl. Yeah, there were a few other chubby kids around, but none as big as I was. I guess you could say I "overshadowed" everyone else. Being the biggest meant I got the most teasing and name calling from the other kids. You know how every classroom has their favorite victim to pick on? I was that favorite from first grade all the way up until eighth. Lucky me. And it didn't help that I could rarely find clothes that fit me so I had to wear black tights and oversized guys' T-shirts pretty much every day throughout elementary school. I wasn't exactly making a fashion statement, even by '90s standards.

By the time I hit fourth grade I was well over 100 pounds and had pretty much heard it all. I had been called everything from the "Pillsbury Doughboy" (a mean boy in my class used to poke me in the stomach and tell me to say "Woo Hoo!") to a "pink cupcake" (I was wearing a pink shirt, and I guess a fat girl in pink looked like a cupcake?) to the all too classic "fatty" (one time a boy ran up to me during PE class just to tell me I was fat—seriously, how rude is that?).

I learned early on that people can be cruel, really cruel. I also learned that if you're fat, or different in any way, you're not cool, pretty, or even likeable. Nobody in my class wanted to be caught socializing with the "fat girl." So I kept to myself and kept quiet. By this time my confidence was so low I was more than willing to accept the fact that no one liked me because of how I looked. I mean, I hated how I looked too! Who was I to be worthy of their attention?

I hadn't always been so self-conscious. Before I even started kindergarten I had a passion for fashion. I would page through my mom's magazines and clothing catalogs from cover to cover, envisioning myself in all the pretty clothes. Dress-up was one of my favorite games to play, and let me tell you, I had an awesome sense of style! My parents have a picture of me wearing a sparkly dress that I had smartly accessorized with a baseball cap and a diaper. I knew all about modeling and looking cute for the camera. I even practiced my "cat walk" in my living room! Being a bit bigger than my sisters and cousins never stopped me from rocking my imaginary runway.

First grade was when I started to see myself as different from everyone else. I noticed that my legs were a little bigger and my tummy a little rounder than most girls and boys in my class. I noticed that running around in PE was a lot harder for me than it was for anyone else. I would get tired and have to stop and walk while my classmates buzzed right past me. And when it was lunchtime, I noticed I could eat more than everyone at my table. My tray would be empty by the time lunch was over. Their trays would still be half full.

And then came the moment when I truly realized there was something wrong with me. It was a typical day at the then-named Buzz Aldrin Elementary School in my hometown of Reston, Virginia. I was sitting at my desk minding my own business, working on my coloring, when a boy in my class walked up to me and informed me he had something to tell me.

"Um," he said, "Matt [not the boy's real name] wanted me to tell you that he wants to marry you . . . when you lose weight."

Boys have such a way with words, don't they? I remember my face flushing. How embarrassing! That was the first time I had been called out for being the chubby girl. In my first grade mind this was a terribly humiliating experience. And it wasn't long before more followed. Matt turned out to be pretty mean (he was the boy who called me the "Pillsbury Doughboy!") and continued to taunt me over the years.

NOT JUST THE KIDS

But kids weren't the only people who noticed my difference in size. Teachers did too. There's one event in particular that I remember. I was waiting in the lunch line next to a girl who was in my class. We were goofing around and wanted to determine how strong we were by seeing how hard we could push each other. She went first and gave me a few hard shoves. When she was done, she told me to push her so we could compare our strength. So I pushed her. But once I did I almost instantly felt a hand wrap around my wrist, and I was dragged out of the lunch line.

The hand belonged to a teacher who had been watching us. He told me that I was not allowed to push other children and that I would get in big trouble if I did it again. Desperate to defend myself, I told him that we were just playing and that she had pushed me too!

"Yes," he said, "but you are bigger than she is and *you* might hurt her."

From that point on I knew school was not going to be a picnic for me. I mean, how much fun could it be if even the *teachers* are picking on you? This definitely didn't do much to bolster my confidence. I became shy and quiet in class, never speaking up unless spoken to. At the ripe old age of eight, I was lonely and depressed.

With no friends, no birthday parties, and no play dates to attend, I spent almost all of my time alone. Fortunately, I loved to read. My time alone was spent poring over pages of books about anything and everything, but my favorites were fantasies. The stories I read about magic and beautiful heroines leading incredible lives, all with happy endings, inspired me to dream.

I can't even tell you how many times I read Patricia C. Wrede's *Dealing with Dragons*. The heroine of the book is a rebel princess named Cimorene, beautiful and brave, who doesn't let anyone tell her what to do, not even dragons. In the story, Cimorene leaves her boring life as a princess in a castle to pursue a life filled with adventure and magic. She struggles through many obstacles (mainly dragons and evil magical creatures who want to eat her) but grows stronger because of them and still gets her prince in the end. If there was any fictional character I would have wanted to trade places with, it was Cimorene.

I wanted a magical life too (but maybe without the dragons), one with a fairy-tale ending. I dreamed of another life, another me, someone who was pretty and had friends and had amazing adventures! Basically, I dreamed of being everything I wasn't. More than anything, though, I dreamed of not being the "fat girl."

That label was what made me different from everybody else. It's what stood between me and the life I wanted. And that's why three weeks before ninth grade started, I went for that walk. I knew the life I wanted to live couldn't happen until *after* I lost weight. I was sick of missing out on things I really wanted to do but felt I couldn't do because I was too big. For example, wearing a bikini at the beach or pool was a definite no-no. Fitting into the cute clothes I saw in magazines and stores was physically impossible. Playing sports or joining a dance class was out of the question too. Please—me lumbering around on a field when I could barely complete one lap around the track? And I would have looked like a dinosaur wearing a leotard and tights. I was fed up with being self-conscious, I was tired of being quiet, and more than anything I was done with being the "fat girl."

FAT GIRL NO MORE

In my last year of middle school, I stood five foot seven inches tall, weighed 230 pounds, and wore a size 20. Today I'm twenty-three, five foot eight inches tall, and 100 pounds lighter, and I wear quite a few sizes smaller. These days boys don't poke my stomach and prompt me to say, "Woo Hoo!"

For a while I didn't think it was anything worth bragging about. To be honest, I was too embarrassed to tell new people I met what I had done. I viewed my weight as an obstacle that was keeping me from my dreams. So I rarely mentioned my 100-pound weight loss. Somehow, though, the subject would come up one way or another. Often because a family member or friend, excited over what I had done, felt as if they must tell everyone they knew. I *hated* when they did this. My whole mission had been to escape the old me and be seen differently. I wanted to forget about being fat! I just wanted to start over as a normal teenage girl. But how could I do that if my fat past kept getting dragged up?

I'm not saying I wasn't excited about losing so much weight. Of course I was! For the first time in my life, I was able to fit into clothing not labeled plus-sized. I could walk into any store and find something I wasn't too big for! Unless you have been shopping at Lane Bryant since the fourth grade, you cannot even imagine how great that felt. Finally, I was done with being the "fat girl." Now I could really start over and live the life I'd always wanted. Why bring up the fact that I used to be a 230-pound middle school loner? That wasn't me anymore, so why did everyone have to know about it?

My fear was that people, especially my peers, would immediately think of me differently once they heard about my past as an obese outcast. For once in my life, I was treated like a normal person. People were not afraid to approach me in fear of "catching my fatness." And I was not afraid of approaching other people in fear of them judging me because of my size. My fear of rejection held me back from building true friendships with the few friends I had made in middle school. But as the weight vanished, so did my fears. Those few friends quickly became my best friends (still are today!), opening me up to a social life like I'd always wanted.

My life was finally going the way I wanted it to go. I had friends and cute clothes (now that I could actually fit into fashionable clothing) and—oh, yeah—boys who actually wanted to talk to me! Things were going so well, I was terrified that if I mentioned my former weight class, I would go from being seen as normal to being seen as freaky and uncool again. Kind of like, once a fat girl always a fat girl? Eventually I got over this fear and realized that I shouldn't be ashamed of who I once was. Besides, who I started out as doesn't define who I am now. The more I got comfortable with my new self, the more I told people about my past. Surprisingly, everyone I told seemed to think what I had done was really amazing.

Apparently, losing a lot of weight was pretty cool. And the more people I told, the more aware I became that for many people (especially girls my age), my weight loss was inspiring. Girls who had heard about what I'd done often asked me for advice. A lot of them were overweight and struggling.

THE WEIGHT-LOSS EQUATION

The words I most often hear after people first learn of my previous "fat girl" incarnation are "What! You? Two hundred and thirty pounds? Are you serious?"

And I can't say I blame them. A 230-pound tween girl losing 100 pounds is not exactly a common story. Even more uncommon is my answer to the question they inevitably ask next.

"Well, what did you do? How did you lose so much weight?"

My answer: "I ate healthy and I exercised."

That's what I tell them because that's what I did. I didn't go on some magical fad diet. I didn't hire a personal trainer. I didn't join a fancy gym. I most certainly did not undergo any surgery. And I definitely did not starve myself. For me that stuff sounded too frustrating, too risky, and too unrealistic. I love a fairy tale as much as anyone, but I knew enough at fourteen to understand that there was no magic spell for weight loss.

Instead I decided to stick to the basics or, perhaps I should say, the obvious. I've never been good at solving equations, but common sense told me that eating less + exercising more = negative amount of fat. It is the natural and proven equation for weight loss that anybody can solve. But apparently a lot of people still don't get it. Every year some $60 billion is spent on weight-loss products and programs. Really, people spend that much money trying to be thin! You would think that with all that money being shoveled out, everyone would be skinny by now. But look around and you'll see that is not the case. And, interestingly enough, Americans are actually getting fatter! Hmm . . . sounds like something is *not* working, but I know for a fact it is not the weight-loss equation.

Maybe it was because I wasn't so caught up in the whole "instant weight-loss diet pills" and "magically slimming" infomercial products that I was able to stick to the math. I mean, I was definitely no expert in health and fitness. I didn't know how long it was going to take to lose 100 pounds. I didn't know how long it would take to lose even one pound! I was clueless about calories and how many I should or shouldn't be eating. The "fat burning" zone on the treadmill meant nothing to me. And what was the deal with healthy carbs versus bad carbs? There was a lot I didn't understand about weight loss. What I did know was that I was done with being fat. I also knew that just *thinking* about changing wasn't going to change anything.

The weight-loss equation was all I had to go on when I first started, and look where that got me! Yet for some reason, a lot of people believe that losing weight requires more than a healthy diet and regular exercise. They think there must be some sort of catch. Surely it's more complicated than that, right? Most of the people I tell about my weight loss are surprised to hear I did it on my own without help from Jenny Craig or gastric bypass surgery.

Why is natural weight loss an unreachable fantasy for so many? Why should anyone assume that I couldn't have lost 100 pounds on my own? I guess most people don't know what can be accomplished with hard work and determination. Want to know a secret that's not really such a secret? If anybody spent an *entire year* working out and eating less, they would lose weight. Not so complicated, right? I didn't think so. Maybe that's why I didn't think my weight loss was such a big deal at first.

IF I CAN DO IT, SO CAN YOU

I began to love seeing the looks on girls' faces when I told them I had done it all on my own. Their eyes would shine bright with surprise and, more importantly, with hope. I knew where they were coming from because I had been where they were—overweight and unhappy. But I hadn't remained that way; I had changed. Now they knew they could too, and without any special surgery or complicated diet program. It made me feel so good when they told me that my story had motivated them to immediately start eating right and exercising. I became aware that my lonely childhood was not so unique. I had not been the only "fat girl" in the world. I'd only felt that way. There are many girls who experienced what I experienced. And there are many more who are even now struggling with their weight issue.

For these girls my story really *is* amazing. Hey, if I can do it, so can they, right? They dream of a better life as a new person but they don't know how to make it happen. Fortunately, I do know how to make it happen, and it is for them (and you, of course)—everyone who shares that same dream—that I decided to write this book.

If you are reading this with the hope I'm going to reveal some secret fat loss trick or gimmicky diet plan, you're going to be disappointed. Like I said, $60 billion is spent on unnecessary diet books and "fat burning pills." Obviously, what I've done did work, and I never spent a dime. In this book I want to show you how it is possible to change your body on your own no matter what your current condition and circumstances are.

At the end of the day, all the latest exercise equipment, great-looking fitness trainers, and doctor certified prepackaged meals don't matter much. You don't need any of that! I didn't have any of that stuff. What I did have was an intense desire to transform my body *and* the determination to make it happen. In my opinion, that's all you need to do most anything.

I hope reading my book will inspire and motivate you to begin changing your life. Why not have the body you want? Why not have the life you want? If it's your dream to be beautiful and fabulous, then don't just sit there thinking about it—do something! If you want to become a marathon runner, start running! Stop holding yourself back and stop hesitating. You've got nothing to lose (except some unwanted fatty tissue). Stop making excuses and make it happen. I know you can. Deep inside, you know it too, don't you? Now, quit wasting time. Change your body and you *will* change your life!

2

Wake-Up Call

The way to get started is to quit talking and begin doing.

—*Walt Disney*

All right, girls, it's time to stop the "I hate my big butt" rants and start whipping those big butts into shape! I know what you are going through—I know how it feels to walk into a trendy clothing store where nothing fits. It feels terrible! But there are two ways you can deal with it. You can be unhappy with your body and wallow in self-pity, forever complaining about your "thunder thighs" *or* you can get mad. Get mad you don't have the body you want. Get mad you can't run one lap around the track without gasping for air. Get mad those skinny brats in school (you know who I'm talking about) think they look better than you. Get mad at the jerks who like to put you down. Get mad that another summer has come and gone and you've yet to don a bikini (at least in public!). Get mad, really mad! Are you angry yet? Good. Make that anger work for you. Let it help you finally shake off the weight that's been smothering your confidence.

Promise yourself that this year is going to be different. This year you won't be turning down any pool party invites; you're going to look forward to them. Be ready to go bikini shopping because that great body you wish you had will be yours!

Just remember, though: *no pain, no gain*. Let's face it, you won't get a great body without putting in some serious effort. What that means is you've got to be willing to change a few things about yourself. First of all, you will need to become a different person. No, I don't mean changing your name or pretending to be someone else. What I mean is you will need to change the things about you that are making you fat.

A WHOLE NEW YOU

Who do you have to become? Someone who sets a goal and doesn't let anything get in the way of reaching it, that's who. Ten pounds won't disappear if you only *plan* on getting healthy. You're going to have to actually put the plan into action! The most effective exercise and diet program on earth will do you no good if you don't have the discipline to complete the program.

Next, you've got to be more positive! Complaining every day about how hard it is to lose weight won't make it happen faster. So what if you don't like sweating? Get used to it. So what if you don't like healthy foods? Suck it up. Stop whining and just do what you know you've gotta do!

Lastly, you've got to bring out your inner confidence and shut out any negativity. Don't let anyone convince you that you won't succeed. Because by summertime the only thing they'll have left to say is "Dang, she looks good!"

This is the mind-set that got me where I am today. When I stopped focusing on how much I hated my body and started thinking about how to make it better, the teasing and taunting I'd endured since elementary school didn't get me down any longer. It just made me want to reach my goal even faster.

My new way of thinking followed me to the gym. All the bottled-up anger and hurt I'd suffered from my tormentors was released. Talk about an energy surge! Those emotions gave me that extra boost of motivation I needed to stick it out when the going got rough. All of the mean glares and hurtful remarks directed at me made me more determined to succeed. Those people wouldn't get the best of me! I promised myself that I wouldn't stop until I reached my goals . . . and I didn't. Now, well, those same rude people don't have much to say about me.

Whit's Tip

Go out and buy (or save money by borrowing from the library) fitness magazines for inspiration. Immerse yourself in the world of health and fitness. That's where you're headed, right? Might as well get an idea of just what your new life is going to look like. Toned bodies and colorful, healthy meals are not such a bad view if you ask me!

TOUGH LOVE

Do you want anyone getting the best of you? No, of course you don't! But they will if you don't get tough and make an attitude adjustment. You might think my advice is a little harsh. I think you've heard enough sugarcoated advice over the years. And in my opinion, most people need a hard shove to get them moving. I think I qualify as the one to give that shove.

Why? Because I've been where you are right now. I am painfully familiar with the life of an overweight child. No doubt your experiences mirror my own. For you, school is a daily humiliation torture chamber. And I bet you've heard your share of fat jokes. As a result, your self-esteem is pretty low. Maybe you feel lonely or left out. Your weight is like a wall between you and everyone else.

If only your life were different. If only you were like the thin girls who wear those little tank tops and miniskirts from Abercrombie. Oh, why can't you be like them? They eat whatever they want and don't worry about gaining weight. It's just not fair! Poor you, why must your life suck so badly?

Then there are those infomercial diet programs you see on TV promising "instant results!" with "no exercise required!" Maybe you try one for about a week and, sadly, it doesn't work. Sigh, well, what do you do now? You just gave it your best shot, didn't you? I mean, you spent *one whole week* trying to lose weight? Yet nothing happened! Oh well, guess you should just go back to eating crap and sitting on your butt.

Ahhh, why couldn't there be some magic pill you could take that would instantly melt away your extra fat. Wouldn't that be great? Just think: you could still stuff your face with greasy, artery-clogging french fries and hamburgers, slurp down syrupy sodas loaded with enough sugar to put you in a diabetic coma (and that, one day, just might), and then, with a simple easy-to-swallow pill, lose weight!

How great would that be? Oh, and the best part is you'd never have to break a sweat. Forget about the treadmill! Why go to the gym when you can spend your time sitting on your butt chatting on Facebook? Hey, if you could lose weight without working out, why even bother with the gruesome task of putting on sneakers? It's not like you need shoes to sit at the computer all day. Ah, wouldn't it be nice if such a pill existed? Well, guess what. It doesn't.

Brace yourself, because this might come as a shock. There is only one way to get rid of fat. How? Burn more calories than you eat. Surprise! That's it. No pills. No surgery. No magic.

What's that? You already know that? Of course, you say, *everyone* knows that—duh! Yeah, yeah, exercise, eat healthy, drink more water, yada yada yada: you've heard it all before. Well then, that's great! You already know what to do, don't you? OK, so why haven't you done it yet? Why are you still complaining about your "thunder thighs"?

I'll tell you why . . . because getting rid of them requires work. You can't get it done all in one day. It takes time, patience, a lot of sweat, and a lot of effort. This is not what you want to hear when you're going on vacation in two weeks? Too bad! The reality is you didn't put on the pounds overnight and you won't lose them overnight either.

Fit Chick Chats

Joemauerishot: Hey, I read your story and I was inspired. I really want to lose weight too! I am about five feet six and 140 pounds. I feel about 5-10 pounds overweight and I really want to lose weight and I would feel so much more comfortable in my body if I lost the weight. Anything you can do to help me would be great. Thank you.

WH: Hi joemauerishot! I totally understand where you are coming from. Even if you are not very overweight, you still know you could be more fit. My advice is to really work on your fitness routine. If you don't have one yet, get one and aim to follow it the best you can. It is sometimes more difficult to lose weight when you don't have as much to lose. This is when you need to focus on ramping up your effort and really pushing yourself. Stay motivated and don't quit, you will get there!

You've got to work hard for a nice body! No one can exercise or eat for you. Those are actions only *you* control. Take charge of your life. Change your eating habits, and get off Facebook and actually move around for once! Stop being lazy and go for that run you keep saying you'll go on! Push yourself and tough out the pain. Losing weight and looking great all depend on what *you* do, and only you.

I know you want to hear that losing weight will be quick and easy, without much effort. You want to see results tomorrow, not next month. You don't want to be patient. Well, OK, keep thinking that way and see where it gets you. Go on wishing your life were different while you devour a tub of chocolate chip ice cream. Maybe you'll get lucky. Maybe you have a fairy godmother who will grant you your wish. With one grandiloquent swish of her wand, she could give you the easy way out, no hard work required. But I wouldn't count on it.

What I've discovered is that wishful thinking is not too helpful. I used to wish I were naturally thin. I wished I would wake up one day to find my days as a "fat girl" were merely a bad dream. I did a lot of wishing, but I never saw any fairy godmother. Nope, I had to make my dreams come true by myself.

And so will you. Sorry, but I did say this was no gimmicky diet book. Transforming your body into bikini-ready is a challenge. If it were so easy, what would be the excuse for anyone to be out of shape?

AN OVERWEIGHT SOCIETY

The fact is there are an awful lot of out-of-shape and overweight people. Did you know that according to the Centers for Disease Control, we are the fattest generation of teenagers and adults to ever walk this earth? No other society in history (except maybe the dinosaurs) has ever been as heavy as we are today. Pretty embarrassing, if you ask me.

But how did this happen? Why have we gotten so fat? And who or what is to blame? The fast food industry? Our schools (cafeteria food, bleh!)? Or maybe we can dump the blame on our parents for allowing us to eat potato chips and drink sodas all day. When you think about it, there is plenty of blame to go around, but blaming someone or something won't make you skinny.

What will start you down the skinny path is recognizing and accepting that even though you are a teenager and still living at home, your life is *your* responsibility. As soon as you realize this, you can no longer blame someone else for your problems. You are who you are right now because of the choices *you* made yesterday, the day before yesterday, and the day before that, and the day before that, and . . . well, you get where I'm going with this. Blaming others for your decisions doesn't change the fact that you made them. Yeah, so maybe it wasn't your fault that your mom made cheesy lasagna and apple cobbler way too often for dinner. But was anyone forcing you to down two or three helpings? And after dinner, wasn't it you who decided to plop down on the couch in front of the TV instead of going for a jog? You are unhappy with your body today because you have been making these kinds of choices day after day, year after year.

Don't get me wrong: I understand that you probably didn't know any better. You were just a kid when you started packing on the pounds. Kids don't understand that ice cream and fistfuls of Girl Scout cookies are unhealthy. I mean, how *would* you know any better if you were never told otherwise? So maybe it is partly your parents' fault that you puffed up. After all, they provided you with the endless amounts of Cap'n Crunch and chicken nuggets. I know my parents sure did.

I didn't know what a calorie was in elementary school. And I most certainly didn't know eating too many of them made you fat. No one ever bothered to discourage me from guzzling three or four helpings at a meal. Food tasted good, so why shouldn't I eat as much as I wanted? In the fourth grade I was a ten-year-old girl who could scarf down as much as a grown man, a large grown man. At my favorite restaurant I would order a huge bacon and cheese hamburger and a mound of french fries, eat the whole meal plus my younger sister's leftovers, and still have enough room for a large slice of chocolate cake.

You might think *someone* would have spoken up or at least tried to get me to eat less but no one ever did. Well, except for one doctor who didn't quite know what to make of an overweight elementary school child. I was in the third or fourth grade. My dad had taken me to the doctor's office because of an earache but Dr. Ross had wanted to talk about something else as well. I guess a nine-year-old girl tipping the scales at nearly 100 pounds was a bit of a shock to her.

"Do you eat more than the other kids at school, Whitney?" she asked me.

"No," I answered quickly. OK, so maybe the truth was that I *did* eat more than the other kids at school. Was it a bad thing to eat more than other people? Something in Dr. Ross's tone suggested it was, and I was not about to tell her the truth.

"Your weight is rather high for someone of your age," she told me.

Well, duh! I had figured that out by this point. Not all of the kids at school were laughed at for their double chin. Being fat was a bad thing; I got it. But what was I supposed to *do* about it? Dr. Ross meant well, of course, but what a way to put someone on the spot! She didn't say anything more about my weight, for which I was grateful. The whole ordeal was very embarrassing for me at that age and did not help me feel any better about my ever-growing size.

My doctor never mentioned my weight again. It wasn't until I entered middle school that I realized on my own just how abnormal and unhealthy my eating habits were. When I finally made the connection, I blamed my parents. Why hadn't they stopped me from eating so much when I was little? Why hadn't they taught me to eat healthier? If they had helped me when I was younger, I likely wouldn't have ended up an overweight and unhappy teenager. In my mind, it was *their* fault, not mine.

It is, after all, the parents' job to look after the health and well-being of their kids. Had my parents bought healthier foods and paid more attention to the amount I was eating, I might not have become overweight. And then maybe I would have been pretty or popular or just simply . . . normal. I knew one thing for sure: had I not been overweight, I would never have suffered through all of the torment and loneliness I'd endured so far.

This realization hit me like a brick. I was hurt and angry with my parents for not stepping in when they could have helped. On a few occasions I lashed out at them, demanding a reason for why they did nothing about my unhealthy weight gain.

Whit's Tip

Maybe your parents don't think leading a healthy lifestyle should be your top priority. Or maybe they think you are being difficult for not eating the same unhealthy stuff they do. If that's the case, start off by explaining to them that you are not in any way trying to make their lives difficult or rebel against their way of life. You are just looking out for your future and trying to do what is best for you. Explain to them why being overweight is negatively affecting your life and that in order for you to lead a happy life, you must make yourself fit and healthy. Tell them how much it would mean to you if they would encourage/support you along the way. But if they do not support your decision, you will continue on your path of health and fitness regardless. Again, remind them you are not rebelling, but simply looking after your own general well-being.

"We didn't know it was going to be such a problem. You ate the same things we all ate," they said once.

With six hungry people all living under one roof, food for us was whatever was cheapest and quickest to prepare. Pizza, fast food, mac 'n' cheese, ice cream, and so on . . . I guess no one in my family was particularly healthy. However, my dad and my two sisters, Hillary and Alana, stayed thin no matter what they ate. My mom, although always thin growing up, became overweight as an adult. My oldest sister, Audra, and I took after my mom. Audra was always a little on the chunky side as a kid, while I was chunky . . . and then some.

Still, couldn't my parents have stopped me from eating so *much* of those foods? I remember how much I ate as a child. I would stuff myself to the point where I would be sick! Terrible stomachaches were the norm for me on a daily basis. You'd think I would learn to avoid stomachaches by not eating so much, but I didn't. Food was just too good! It was addicting and no one told me to stop, so I didn't.

My parents' explanation was not quite what I was hoping to hear, but it's what I got. I had one final question: why didn't they make me exercise more when I was little? That might have helped at least a little bit! I was a pretty inactive kid most of the time. Then again, what kid wants to go outside when cartoons are playing on the TV nonstop? Besides, there was not much for me to do outside. The neighborhood we lived in didn't have a lot of kids to play with. My older sisters never wanted me around their friends, and Alana was just a baby. Unless I wanted to play peekaboo with my infant sister, I was out of luck. Still, couldn't my parents have made me do *some* form of exercise? Not that it mattered much at this point anyhow. No answer they could give me would have made me any less fat.

TAKING RESPONSIBILITY

My middle school years were pretty rough. From the sixth to the eighth grade, I moped around feeling sorry for myself, blaming my parents, and hating my body. Guess where that got me? Not far at all. While I was busy feeling sorry for myself and playing the blame game, I continued with my unhealthy lifestyle. I hated how I looked, and I wanted to be healthy and happy, but I didn't do anything about it. I wanted to be a different person, but I didn't do anything differently. I was still making the same choices I had always made, the choices that made me overweight and unhappy in the first place.

What I should have realized then was that I was the only one to blame. Even when I knew my lifestyle was the reason I was overweight, I still did nothing. It took me nearly three years to finally accept that blaming my parents was not going to make me skinny or happy. From that point on I knew it was up to me to change my life. The choices I made from then on would determine whether I would be the "fat girl" for the rest of my life or the girl I wanted to be. No more blame game. This time it all depended on me, just me.

Do you get it yet? The only person who can change your life is *you*. Whether you'll end up with the body you want all depends on what *you* do from this moment forward. So, what's your next move going to be?

Whit's Tip

Announce to your friends and family you are going to lose weight. Go on—put this book down and pick up the phone. Call all of your friends, your cousins, your parents, your grandparents, whoever. And if they don't answer, run across the street and tell your neighbor if you have to! This is an exciting new step for you, one that will change your life. Letting your friends and family know about your new undertaking will help keep you in check. Because once they know about it, they won't waste any time calling you out if they see you slack. Don't give them the chance to! Prove to them you can and will stick by your life-changing decision.

TAKING ACTION

The number one reason you're still fat is that you haven't yet made the *decision* to change your life; you haven't yet made the *decision* to lose weight. The longer you wait, the longer you are missing out on the life you could be living. The clock is ticking. Why spend a moment longer in a body you don't want? Start now, right now! Don't wait. I waited fourteen years before I took action, but who knows where I would be now if I had acted earlier? Trust me on this: the longer you wait, the more you'll regret not starting earlier. And what *are* you waiting for? No time is better than the present, so get a move on!

Are you listening? I mean now! Put this book down and go for a fifteen-minute walk. Go outside, hop on a treadmill, walk back and forth in your living room, or walk in place if you have to—just start moving! Do fifty jumping jacks or do some push-ups and sit-ups. Do anything. It doesn't matter what you do; the point is to take action now, this very moment. Don't wait until sometime in the future. Do something now!

Well, did you? Did you take my advice? Did you put this book down and get up and move? If you did, great! You just moved one step closer to reaching your goal. If you didn't, why not? What could you possibly be waiting for? You do want to change, don't you?

Any action, no matter how small, will move you toward your goal. Don't only think about how you want your body to look; think about how to make it happen! Once you have an idea, get right to it. No more waiting, just doing.

I immediately acted on changing my life by simply taking a walk, and look where I am now—a confident young woman, a fashion model, and a first-time author. Who knew that walk would lead to such an outcome? Since then I haven't stopped taking action. I'm moving closer and closer to my many goals. I know for a fact that sitting around thinking about doing something someday in the future doesn't make it happen. What does make it happen is diving straight into action.

Really, any positive step you take toward your goal has an impact. For example, choosing to withhold the whipped cream on your daily coffee drink might not seem like a huge step. But skipping out on the whipped cream every day means you're skipping out on the extra calories too. The absence of those calories in your diet will lead to less fat in your body. And that's by simply cutting out whipped cream. Imagine what would happen if you made even more of those small changes. Yep, a lot would happen.

3

Goals

If one advances confidently in the direction of his dreams, and endeavors to live the life which he has imagined, he will meet with a success unexpected in common hours.

—Henry David Thoreau

Quick—name five goals you have for this year! Uh-oh, what's that? You can't think of any? Hmm . . . then you've got a problem. How do you expect to get anything you want if you don't even know what you want? OK, sure, you know you want to lose weight, but you've got to be just a tad more specific than that. Setting goals is really, really important, maybe even *the* most important factor in weight loss. Why? Well, first let me tell you a little story about goals.

THE LIST

Sometime midway through my eighth-grade year, my dad told me about this guy who made a list of 100 things he wanted to do in his lifetime. He wrote them down in a journal and looked at his list nearly every day. Soon enough he noticed that opportunities for him to fulfill his goals started to appear. He continued reading his list every day and crossing them off as he did them. By the end of his life he had accomplished all 100 of his written goals. I thought this story was so cool. It amazed me that this man actually did everything he put on his list. And something else amazed me. It seemed like just because he *wrote* his goals down, they happened for him. Now that was something I knew I had to try for myself. There were a lot of things I wanted to do and if writing them down worked for him, maybe it would work for me.

The same night I found an empty journal and began writing my own list of lifelong goals. At the top I wrote:

Run one mile without stopping.

Lose weight and be healthy throughout my life.

Then I went wild and wrote down everything I had ever wanted to do, trying to leave out nothing. There were places I wanted to visit: Paris, Italy, China, New York City, Africa, and more. There were random things I wanted to do: dig for dinosaur bones, go on a ghost hunt, attend a ball. I listed the names of people I wanted to meet and crazy dreams I rarely shared with anyone, such as becoming a model and an actress. When I finished my list of goals, I ended up having a lot more than 100.

I planned on doing everything on my list, but running a full mile and losing weight was where I wanted to start. At my school, everyone was required to run a mile twice a year in PE. It was part of the dreaded physical fitness tests. We were graded on how many sit-ups, push-ups, and pull-ups we could do. What's worse is that after we did them, our teacher made us say our scores out loud in front of the entire class. Reluctantly I'd announce my low numbers in a quiet voice (although sometimes I cheated and said I did more than I really did!). It was horribly shameful.

We were also graded on how fast we could run one mile. Unfortunately, I couldn't cheat on my mile time. Needless to say, I was no cheetah. Twice every year I was subjected to the utter embarrassment of being the last one to finish. My classmates stared as I lumbered along, huffing and puffing, finally reaching the finish line a good ten minutes after everyone else. I absolutely despised physical fitness tests.

Whit's Tip

Think about your fitness goals right now! Brainstorm in your journal at least three fitness goals you want to achieve someday. The amount of weight you want to lose would of course be a good one to start with, but what else? Do you want to gain more muscle? (Yes, you do!) Do you want to be a healthier eater? (Yup!) Do you want to be able to run faster or play tennis really well? What is it exactly that you want your body to be able to do? Think about it for a minute and then start writing them down in your journal. Look over your goals every day. The more you focus on them, the faster you'll accomplish them!

For that reason, running a mile without stopping was number one on my list. My goal was to run that mile with ease and to finish at a normal time, just like my 90-pound classmates.

Losing weight was next on my list. Many of my dreams wouldn't even be possible unless I was in shape. (Yeah, climbing the Great Wall of China with 100 pounds of extra "baggage"? Not happening.) It was the bridge between me and my other goals.

Writing that list soon led to an entire year of journal entries. Almost every day I was writing something. Meaning, every day my goals stared me in the face. But still, I didn't seem to be accomplishing any of them—until a few weeks before ninth grade started.

ACHIEVING GOALS

On that summer afternoon when I made the decision to get my lazy butt up off the couch, the bridge between me and my goals was crossed. It took about a year to cross the darn thing, but once it was done I had lost 100 pounds and could run well over one mile. And those were just my first two goals.

At 100 pounds lighter I felt pretty for the first time in my life. Modeling was still a dream I kept to myself, but why keep it a secret any longer? I wanted to be a model, so I sent photos of myself to a few modeling contests. I didn't win all of them, but I placed in a few. That's better than nothing, right? And I did get my picture in *Seventeen* magazine for being one of the best-tressed girls in America, which was totally awesome! I'd never thought much of my hair, but hey, if *Seventeen* wanted it in their pages, I was more than willing to oblige!

With my newfound confidence I was eager to try almost anything and mark more goals off my list. That year my school was participating in a student exchange program to Austria. Since I was a little kid, I'd dreamed of traveling to foreign countries and here was an opportunity to do so! I jumped at the chance to go. Spending a week in Austria was a spontaneous move for me, because I never would have gone if I were still trapped in my old body. But I was turning into a new person now, inside and out.

Opportunities were popping up left and right. I'd put "learn how to box" on my list because I thought it would be fun to try. I almost forgot it was on there until an LA Boxing gym opened just fifteen minutes from where I lived. I had my dad take me to check it out, and I signed up that very day. Check! Yet another goal accomplished.

As things kept happening for me, I found it kind of eerie that goals written down the year before were actually coming true. Why did ically writing down my goals seem to work better than only thinking them? I didn't know, but I sure wasn't going to complain! Especially checked off one of my most desired goals—Paris. From the time

I was a little girl, I had been in love with France: the food, the language, and, of course, Paris. In my junior year of high school, my art teacher announced she was taking a group with her to France for a class trip. Of course I had to go!

While in Paris I couldn't believe I was really there! My longtime dream of visiting the most beautiful city in the world had come true. And I was there all because I decided to change my life on that hot summer day two years before. I believe that when I acted on one of my dreams, my other dreams began coming true too. They just needed a little push to get going.

Now, by far the most exciting event I've experienced since losing weight was appearing on the *Oprah Winfrey Show*. Yes, I was on *Oprah!* I can't say that being on *Oprah* was one of the goals on my list. It was more of a surprise bonus goal come true! And again, it all had to do with my written goal, my second one. In the fall of my junior year, my parents persuaded me to write a letter to Oprah about my weight loss. A few months later I got a call from Harpo Studios. A producer told me Oprah was doing an episode on teen obesity and weight-loss surgery. She asked me if I would like to appear on the show as the only teen who did *not* have surgery to lose weight.

Did I want to be on the *Oprah Show?* Uh . . . *yeah*! Three weeks later my parents and I were on a plane to the Windy City. We had never been to Chicago before, and we were excited to visit the home city of the famous *Oprah Winfrey Show*. I immediately fell in love with Chicago. My favorite experience (besides meeting Oprah, of course!) was sitting in the restaurant at the top of the John Hancock building. We sat ninety-something stories above the street, enjoying a breathtaking view of the city and Lake Michigan. Well, my dad and I were enjoying the view. My mom is afraid of heights. You might say she was a little uncomfortable. It was snowing, and from that height the city looked like an enchanted winter wonderland. I decided then and there I would visit Chicago again.

The afternoon I met Oprah, I was more nervous than excited. I was afraid that when she interviewed me on camera I would mess up and look like an idiot. But it was too late to back out! Soon I was ushered to my seat and the show began. When Oprah walked onstage in her bright orange sweater, I was starstruck. Literally. I couldn't stop staring. I mean, it was Oprah! Nervously, I waited while she talked to the other teenage guests. They told her their stories of being the "fat kid" and how much they hated it. They claimed they had tried everything but nothing worked. Surgery was the only option for them.

Listening to their stories, I found myself wondering whether they really *had* tried everything. I mean, they all claimed they ate the same foods they ate prior to the surgery. The only difference now was, thanks to their gastric bypass surgery, they had to eat smaller portions. Well, if they had only eaten less to begin with, they would have lost weight without the surgery, right? Yet they said they had done *all* they could. Hmm . . . something just didn't add up.

I didn't have much time to think about it, though, because soon enough Oprah's attention was focused on me. Again, I was starstruck. Oprah was looking at me! Ahhh! I was really sweating now. Then she spoke to me (Oprah Winfrey speaking to me?!) and surprisingly, I was able to form coherent sentences and answer all of her questions. I swear that woman must have special powers or something.

Whit's Tip

What about your dreams? If my only goal was to look good in a bathing suit, I might not have come as far as I have today. My reasons for losing weight went beyond just wanting to be skinny. I had bigger dreams that I wanted to make happen; those were my main motivation. What do you dream about doing someday in your new body? Who is the person you have always wished you could be? Now is the time to write down your own dreams and take the first step toward making them a reality.

SEEING IS BELIEVING

Are you beginning to see why goals are so important? Do I really need to tell you to write down your own goals? OK, I'll tell you again just in case—write down your goals! Write them all down, each and every one of them. An imaginary list in your head isn't good enough. Writing down what you want to accomplish keeps you focused and helps you do it faster.

Whit's Tip

Instead of a vision board, you could make a vision collage on your wall or on the back of your bedroom door. You could also make a virtual vision board on your computer and use it as a screensaver.

I kept a journal throughout my entire weight loss (still do) and really believe it was a crucial factor in my success. Now I want you to do the same! If you don't have a blank journal at home, you can buy one (try Walmart or the dollar store to get one cheap) or even make one by stapling together regular copy paper (I've done this before; it works!). Use this same journal for everything I ask you to write down later on in the book. But first things first: use it to write down all of your goals.

Having a tangible, written list of your goals is your reminder to get them done! Put your journal where you can easily get to it. Read your goals every day and repeat them to yourself over and over. Every night I write in my journal and read through my goals. Rarely will you find me without a pen and a pad of paper nearby.

Vision boards are another strategy that helps you keep your focus. A vision board is a collage of your goals and dreams. Basically, it is everything you wrote down on your list but in picture format. What images come to mind when you think about yourself fit and thin? Flip through magazines or go on the internet and find pictures that match your ideal body or that inspire you. You can even draw something if you're the creative type. Maybe there is a particular celebrity or athlete whose body you admire. Print their pictures, cut them out, paste them on a poster board, and voilà! There is your vision board.

You can put whatever you want on your board. I have so much on mine that I use two. One is for my lifelong goals, and the other is for my fitness goals. Both boards are placed on the wall right across from my bed. This way every morning and every night I have pictures of my to-do list staring me down. They keep me motivated to continue working toward my goals.

There is a lot of truth in the statement "seeing is believing." When you see visual images of your goals, you are much more likely to achieve them. If you make your goals your primary focus, they'll happen. I promise.

4

Motivation

People say motivation doesn't last. Well, neither does bathing—that's why we recommend it daily.

—*Zig Ziglar*

When was the last time you felt really motivated to do something? I hope it was when you picked up this book and decided to lose weight! I'm going to pretend I didn't hear you say it was when you did your friend's homework in return for a visit to Cold Stone Creamery. In any case, remember that crazy energy that impelled you to jump immediately into the task? Remember how nothing else mattered as much as what you were motivated to do?

Can't think of any time you were this pumped? Then pretend your parents said to you, "We'll give you five thousand dollars to clean your room." How would you feel then? What would be the first thing you'd do? Unless you are incredibly lazy (or incredibly rich), I'm pretty sure you'd clean your room, maybe even the entire house while you were at it!

Now pretend someone told you, "You can have the body of your dreams—flat stomach, lean legs, toned arms—and all you have to do is exercise a few times a week and eat a little better." Put like that, getting in shape doesn't sound all that difficult, does it? That's because it isn't. Getting a healthy body is a simple and straightforward process. It is only difficult if you make it so. Kind of like cleaning your room is difficult. Folding clothes, making the bed, vacuuming your floor. Ugh. Not exactly exciting. But throw in an offer of $5,000 and those lukewarm feelings heat up real fast. Suddenly, cleaning your room sounds like a great idea! Every cell in your body tingles with excitement as you smooth your bed covers and collect dirty clothes off the floor. You might even find it isn't as difficult or time consuming as you'd expected it to be. In fact, you might enjoy the task (OK, maybe that's going too far). After all, your mind was only focused on the *result* of cleaning your room—you know, that major shopping spree. Yep, $5,000 seems like a pretty good return for simply folding a few shirts and making up your bed.

Kind of how a great body is a pretty swell reward for simply exercising and eating healthy. I hope the idea of losing layers of unhealthy fat *forever* excites you as much as, if not more than, the idea of being handed $5,000. Believe me: your dream body is worth much, much more than a shopping spree.

Losing weight is the *result* of living a healthy lifestyle. Being fat is the result of an unhealthy lifestyle. Your body functions at its best when you eat nutritious foods and keep your body active. Yeah, I know—guzzling carrot juice and dancing to cardio burn workout DVDs don't sound all that appealing to you. Not yet anyway. I mean, you're so accustomed to scarfing down Oreos and Pringles while zoning out for hours watching TV that exercise is the last thing on your mind. You're stuck in your comfort zone of doing what you've always done. Apparently, though, what you've been doing sucks, because you're not happy, are you? Which means it's time to break out of your comfort zone. How do you do that? Get motivated!

MOTIVATION—FICKLE FRIEND

You see, it is motivation that impels you to take action and keep on taking action. It's what sparks the fire and fuels your desire. Drastically changing your lifestyle will require a lot of motivation. You probably have plenty of good reasons to lose weight, and thinking about them is exciting. But that feeling doesn't always last, does it? You start out feeling super pumped and then, after only a couple of weeks, the passion fades.

Whit's Tip

Don't think of working out or eating healthy as a chore. Think of every workout and every healthy meal as an opportunity to get closer to your goal! The sooner you start, the closer you'll be to your dream body.

I'm sure you know what I'm talking about. Maybe one time you decided you were finally going to get in shape. All fired up, you slipped on a pair of sneakers and off you went for a jog. It was probably hard, but you were so motivated you didn't care, and kept going. Afterward you felt great! Yep, you were really going to do it this time—you were going to be flab free in time for your family's summer vacation. At that moment you vowed to run every day.

The next day rolled around and, still brimming with enthusiasm, you went for another run. Again, the run made you feel great, and again you vowed to run the next day.

Well, the next day arrived, but this time you hesitated—so much homework to do, you just didn't think you'd be able to squeeze it in. That's OK, you could do it tomorrow. Sure, there was always tomorrow.

But tomorrow came around and you were feeling kind of tired. So maybe this one time you'd take a break, though definitely the next day you would run for sure.

Uh-huh.

The next day you still didn't feel like running. So you took another break . . . and another . . . and another, and before you knew it you'd completely forgotten about your vow to run every day. Soon you were back to staring like a zombie at the TV. Back to devouring bags of Fritos and containers of fried rice. You were back to being the person you don't want to be.

Does this sound familiar? This is what so many people go through again and again. They start out thinking they can lose 10 pounds by Friday, but they aren't willing to stick with the program long enough to see major changes. Then they wonder why they failed.

Fit Chick Chats

blockerbabae14: Hey Whit!! Okay, I read your story, and I can totally relate! I'm not overweight, but I am bigger than all the girls in my grade, and most of the girls on the volleyball court! I want to be able to wear a bikini this summer and not feel self-conscious about myself! I lost a lot of weight two years ago, and I want to lose another 15 to 20 lbs this year, and guess what? I'm totally committed now! You completely inspired me!

WH: Hi blockerbabae14! Yay! I'm glad you are motivated to go after your goals. The first step is to start! I wish you the best!

Well, losing 10 pounds will take longer than a week. The problem is that many stop trying after only a week or two. But just think where all those people would be if they hadn't stopped. Where would you be if you had stayed motivated? If you ran every day like you planned on doing, you wouldn't be lugging around those jiggling pounds now. You know I'm right, but how do you stay motivated long enough to reach your goal?

KEEP THE MAGIC ALIVE

Let's talk about your mind-set again. Discipline will only get you so far; you've also got to have both desire and belief. What I mean is, you must *really* want to change your body, so much so that you'll do whatever it takes. Until you are 100 percent ready to do that, don't waste your time trying. Looking bikini-ready won't happen overnight and it will take a lot of work. Sorry, but taking your dog for a walk once a week or eating an apple every now and then isn't going to cut it. You'll need to put in more effort than that, but if you have enough desire to change, you'll do it.

Whit's Tip

I was lucky enough to be born with an optimistic disposition. There was always a voice in my head that broke through my negative thoughts of "I can't" and told me "I can." You can adopt your own "I think I can" voice. Think of all the things you've told yourself you can't do. Examples: *I can't lose weight. I can't give up junk food. I can't stick to a regular workout schedule.* Whenever you catch yourself thinking this way, immediately stop and replace "I can't" with "I can." Examples: *I can lose weight if I eat healthy and exercise. I can give up junk food if I strengthen my self-discipline day after day. I can stick to a workout schedule if I make exercise my top priority.* Come on, try it! Say it out loud and repeat saying "I can" as many times as it takes for you to drown out the "I can't" voice.

And as corny as it sounds, you must believe in yourself. There is nothing more unmotivating than worrying you won't be able to do it, it will be too hard, or it will take too long. You'll waste all of your time doubting yourself when that time could be better spent working toward your goal.

Believe that you can do something and convince yourself it's possible and you'll find there is a lot you are capable of.

Do this right now. Picture yourself 10, 20, or 30 pounds lighter. You feel excellent, right? Now imagine failing. Picture yourself a year from now still eating potato chips in front of the TV. How does *that* make you feel? Terrible, so don't ever think about it! Erase any thoughts of failing. Only see yourself succeeding!

I've learned that when you expect to reach your goal, you will. When I was fourteen, I was serious about losing exactly 100 pounds. There was no possibility of failure for me because I just never thought about it. All I did think about was how much better my life would be once I lost the weight. I expected to succeed. Period.

Not that dropping 100 pounds was peaches and cream all the time. I got discouraged now and then. Those were the days when I felt my goal was impossible.

One such moment happened after I had lost around 40 pounds. Since shedding that much weight, I felt pretty good about myself. I was wearing new clothes because my old ones didn't fit (yay!), and I already had more confidence. For the first time school was exciting, because I actually felt like I fit in. But I forgot that losing 40 pounds off my 230-pound frame meant I was still w-a-y overweight.

My friend and I were at a pep rally in our school's gym. We were walking up the bleachers looking for a place to sit. The aisles were crowded, so there was not a lot of room to move. All of a sudden I lost my balance and started to sway back and forth. For a moment it appeared I was going to topple over on top of two guys seated below me. Aware of my impending wipeout, they put their hands out to try to help me catch my balance. Fortunately, I found my footing and managed not to fall on them.

My friend and I continued to shuffle to seats not far above the boys. I noticed they were laughing and I tuned in to what they were saying. It went something like this:

"Wow, she would have crushed us if she had fallen."

The other boy snickered and said, "Why can't people just *lose* weight?"

That stung me big time. Right then my confidence crumbled. Here I was feeling I wasn't so big, that I looked pretty good and not all that different from everyone else. Well, obviously I had thought wrong.

Their comments stayed with me for the rest of the day and the next and the next. Who was I kidding? Sure, I had lost some weight, but I was far from normal. I was still the "fat girl." The more I thought about it, the more angry I felt. Sure, I felt pretty bad about the boys' remarks, but I wasn't going to allow a few insensitive comments to stop me. Nope, instead I got really mad. Those jerks wouldn't get the best of me. I worked out harder and ate even better. I used that kick in the gut as motivation to reach my goal faster.

Whit's Tip

Pick up your journal again, and this time brainstorm all of the times you've felt slighted, been harassed, or told you could not do something because of your size. Don't use this as a time to reflect on how horrible your life has been so far and then go grab a bowl of ice cream to drown your sorrows. Stop that! Use this opportunity to add more fuel to your fire! How dare other people treat you like that? Who do they think they are to put you down? Wouldn't you like to prove them wrong? Wouldn't you like to show all of your tormentors just how powerful you are? Of course you would, and you will. Look back at this list whenever you feel like you need that extra push. Remember, success is the best revenge.

Other times I was down because of my own doing. After weeks and months of trying to eat healthy, there were moments when I cracked. Generally, it would happen after some occasion where sweets and salty snacks were a free-for-all. I would try to resist the temptation and not eat any. On good days this would work, but not every day was good. On bad days I convinced myself that one bite wouldn't hurt. I promised myself I would take only one bite and then stop but that was never the case. One bite soon turned into an all-out binge on whatever was in front of me. Later, I would feel so bad and be so angry with myself that I would head to the kitchen and binge-eat some more. It was a vicious cycle that would go on for days.

During these crazy out-of-control periods, I was fully aware I was sabotaging my weight-loss efforts. I knew I was hurting myself. Talk about frustrating! It was hard to get back on track when I felt like I'd just ruined everything. But to get focused again, I had to put aside my guilt. The past is in the past and that's where it should stay. Just like with the jerks at school, my setbacks pushed me to work harder.

What I realize now is that every one of my low moments made me stronger. Because every time I was down, I had to use more strength to get back up. My burning determination to succeed, to lose the weight, would pull me through. And I never let go of the vision of myself succeeding. Obviously I didn't feel very successful at times, but even during those gloomy periods, I never lost sight of my ultimate goal. Expect to accomplish your goals and you will. Remember this especially when you reach your own low moments.

VISUALIZATION

Maybe this will help: Imagine strolling on a beach, wearing a cute bikini, feeling completely comfortable with your body, and knowing you look good! No more hiding your belly underneath oversized T-shirts and claiming you don't want to get sunburned. Nope, that's not you anymore. Now you're lean and mean, with a body to kill for. That confident hottie strutting her stuff on the beach is you!

It's an exciting thought, isn't it? Ahh yes, imagine never turning down another hot tub party invite. You're probably itching to hit the gym right now. No? Then you need to work on your imagination. Take the time to create an image in your mind of yourself at your goal weight. Imagine not only what you will look like but also how you will feel. Will you feel lighter, more energetic, happier, and more confident? What clothes will you wear, and what activities will you do when you are in shape?

Visualize your ideal self as often as possible. The more you do, the more you'll want to make that image a reality. Soon turning down a slice of cake will no longer seem like such a big deal because you'll be seeing your slim, healthy body in your mind's eye. When you truly want something, you will do whatever it takes to get it. A few hours a week of sweating at the gym and switching french fries for an apple are small prices to pay for a healthy, hot figure.

Now, are you willing to give up an hour in front of the television for an hour (or less) at the gym? Of course you are! Are you willing to replace your greasy beef fried rice takeout meal with a fresh vegetable stir-fry? You bet!

Of course, there will be days, usually those cold, rainy days, when the thought of just getting out of bed, let alone working out, doesn't sound the least bit appealing. These are the days when you consider skipping out on your workout, promising yourself you'll do it *tomorrow*. And then, as I mentioned earlier, you'll push it off again and again until eventually you stop altogether. Believe me when I say I know it is hard to be motivated when all you want to do is curl up and watch Disney movies. But get over it! Moving is exactly what you must do.

GET MOVING

Force yourself to snap out of your lazy mood. Think about how good you will feel after you complete your workout and how bad you will feel if you don't. Push through it; you can rest when it's over! Try to get excited about your workouts. Remember why you're doing them in the first place. The amount of calories and fat you'll burn? Pretty good deal if you ask me!

Then change into your gym clothes and do a quick warm-up. Even when you feel dead tired, throwing yourself into motion will wake up your muscles and energize your body. Warming up always gets me in the mood to exercise. Music helps too. I blast some Bon Jovi or Lady Gaga and then do a bunch of jumping jacks and a few sit-ups, push-ups, and squats. That way I get the blood running through every muscle group.

MISSION POSSIBLE

Another trick I use is setting a "mission" for myself. This way I feel I have more of a purpose for not skipping out on my workout. When I was training for my first Walt Disney World Marathon, I used this strategy to get me through my runs. Running a marathon is exhausting, so I knew I had to train hard! Nearly every day I ran. I was building up to more miles so I'd be ready to run the full 26.2 miles on race day. If I missed a training run, I would be behind schedule and probably wouldn't make it through the entire race. It was tough waking up every weekend knowing a ten-, fifteen-, or twenty-mile run lay ahead of me, but I made it my one goal for the day, a "mission" to complete. Each training run was a new mission. All else would wait until that run was done. But once I completed my mission, I was free to do whatever. And the feeling of accomplishment was never better!

Set your own "missions." The next time you find yourself wanting to cozy up on the couch instead of working out, remember your mission, whatever that might be, like doing two more push-ups or running a little farther or faster than you're used to. Make it your main priority for the day. Everything else can wait.

Once you complete your mission, you'll feel accomplished and ready to try it again or start a new mission. Each time you complete a challenge you are closer to walking down that beach in your bikini. All it takes is a little motivation to get you started.

FIND SUPPORT

Hey, I get it. Some things are easier said than done. You can visualize dropping bullies in dunk tanks all you want or think so positively that unicorns and rainbows practically shoot out from your ears. But that might not always be enough. We all have our own stories and our own obstacles to overcome, some more difficult than others. There is no shame in admitting that you might not be strong enough yet to face your toughest battle on your own. Sometimes you need help to get you started and there is nothing wrong with asking for it.

In that case start looking for someone who can offer help and support. Parents, as much as we love them, may not always be your best option. Let's face it. Sometimes parents *just don't get it*—right? If that's the case, look for help elsewhere. Friends can sometimes be great people to talk to but not necessarily the best advisors if they lack experience in your situation.

Look for a more mature support system. Maybe you have an older sibling, an aunt, uncle, grandparent, or trusted family friend you could talk to. If not, maybe look to your guidance counselor at school. He or she might be able to offer you the guidance you need or refer you to someone who can. Another idea would be to ask around or look online to see if there is a support group nearby that you could join. Whatever kind of help you need, there are lots of people out there willing to give it. It might take some time to find just the right person, but believe me, he or she is out there! Or to talk to me, go to whitneyholcombe.com and ask me anything you want.

GET MOTIVATED!

I've already told you the reasons I was so motivated to lose weight. But this book is written for you and now it's your turn to tell me what inspires you.

Write it down: Get out your journal and write down every reason you so badly want to lose weight. Is it because you want to join the soccer team? Look great in a bikini? Fit into that gorgeous homecoming dress you saw at the mall? Whatever your reasons, write them down! Think about all the things that make you want a healthy body more than anything.

1. **Why does it matter?:** Now that you are excited about your reasons for losing weight, write down why those reasons are so important. What about you or your life would change if you got on the soccer team or could fit into that dress? Do you think you would be happier, more confident, more outgoing? How would losing weight affect the people and events in your life?

2. **Make the sacrifice:** Losing a lot of weight will take time and patience. How quickly you see results will depend on how much you have to lose, but also on the amount of effort you put into it. The harder you push, the faster you get your dream body. So, how hard are you willing to push? What sacrifices are you willing to make? Maybe it will mean getting up early to do a workout before you go to school. Maybe you will need to go outside your comfort level and turn that walk into a jog. It will most definitely mean giving up chocolate fudge sundaes as a midnight snack! Remember, you may make these sacrifices grudgingly at first, but you'll be glad you did when the results start showing. Now write down those sacrifices you're willing to make.

3. **One year:** All right, so you've thought about why you want to lose weight, what will change once you do, and what you'll have to give up to do so. Now here comes the challenge. I am giving you one year to get to your goal weight. However much you've got to lose, it is now your mission to do whatever you must to get there in one year. More specifically, you'll do whatever is *healthy*. Don't you dare let me find you hanging your head over a toilet after every meal. Besides

being a totally unnatural (and disgusting!) way to lose weight, bulimia is also harmful to your health. Gum disease, ulcers, anemia, dry skin, even heart problems are all effects bulimia can have on the body. Harming yourself in order to reach a goal is never the way to go. Especially since the healthy way is more effective—and sanitary! Now, let's get back to the one-year challenge. Of course, if you have more than 100 pounds to lose you'll need more time, but see how much you *can* lose in that period.

4. **Accept the challenge:** Do you accept the challenge? Are you ready to get started right this instant? Great! Tell me you're willing; tell me you can do it. Write this down in your journal now!

> I, ________________, accept the challenge to try my best to reach my goal weight in one year's time. I am ready and willing to do whatever it takes to healthily change my body and my life.

Well, it's official now. There is no turning back. Looks like you only have 365 days to complete the challenge. If I were you, I'd get to it!

5

Habits

First we form habits, then they form us. Conquer your bad habits, or they'll eventually conquer you.

—Dr. Rob Gilbert

You say you want a great body, wonderful! But what have you done about it so far? From the moment you decided to lose weight, that was your cue: the choices you make every day must change. You cannot be a healthy person if you eat poorly. You cannot have a lean and toned body if you do not exercise. You cannot expect to lose weight if you do not act like someone who wants to lose weight.

How do you do that? By changing your bad habits (the ones that got you where you are today) into the habits of a fit and thin person. What healthy people do everyday keeps them looking good. So wouldn't you want to follow their example?

Whit's Tip

Right now, make a change. Do something, anything differently from what you do on a daily basis. Rearrange the furniture in your room; get rid of old clothes, toys, papers, whatever you don't need; wear your hair differently . . . Not every change you make must be fitness related (although it couldn't hurt if it was!). Making any kind of change will prove you are willing to become a new person who is willing to do things differently. Change is like a chain reaction. Make even one small change, and other areas of your life will begin to change as well.

HABIT REFORM

When I first started changing my habits, I wasn't sure I would ever get used to them. How could one go without waffles, pastries, and doughnuts? And no more french fries every afternoon in the school cafeteria? Plus, how in the world was I going to make myself go to the gym after school on an almost daily basis when all I wanted to do was crash on my couch and watch TV until bedtime?

The idea of giving up my favorite foods and forcing myself to be active every other day seemed unappealing and nearly impossible. But my desire to change was stronger than my addiction to junk food and reality TV show reruns. Changing my body meant changing my habits.

Habit Reform #1: Eating Breakfast

From everything I'd read and heard about weight loss, eating breakfast seemed to be pretty important. I'd read that eating within the first hour of waking up kick-starts your metabolism for the day and satiates your hunger until lunchtime. That way you will be less likely to overeat in the afternoon.

I never ate breakfast in the morning because I never had enough time to get ready *and* eat. Come lunchtime, I was famished. I'd eat anything and everything I could fit on my cafeteria tray! But now weight loss was my priority. If that meant getting up a few minutes earlier in order to eat breakfast, then that's what I would have to do.

When I began eating breakfast every morning, I noticed right away that I had better control over my appetite in the afternoon. The more control I had over my appetite, the more control I had over my junk food cravings. This was a crucial first step for me getting on a healthy weight-loss track. It was also one of the easiest habits to adopt.

Habit Reform #2: Healthier Food Choices

I knew things like pizza, hamburgers, and french fries were not good for me and were not good for weight loss. Guess what was on the daily school cafeteria menu? Yep, all of the above and more. Luckily, the cafeteria also offered a few other choices like salads and turkey sandwiches with sides of fruit or vegetables. It took me a while to build up my discipline enough to bypass every unhealthy item in the cafeteria line. French fries were the hardest; they just smelled *so* good!

But week after week my discipline grew stronger and my tray began filling with healthier foods. Eventually I opted out from buying lunch at school to waking up even earlier to pack my own healthy lunch. My lunch habits followed me outside school into restaurants, home, and wherever food was offered. It became second nature for me to automatically choose the healthiest option on the menu. I'm still this way now, and it has definitely paid off!

Habit Reform #3: Workout Time

When I got home from school, the last thing I wanted to do was hit the gym. Sitting for hours at school left me drained, tired, hungry, and unmotivated to do much of anything. I would push off my scheduled workout until later . . . which turned into even later . . . which turned into too late to possibly get in a workout!

I knew I was slacking, and I knew that slacking wouldn't help me lose 100 pounds. So, I made a change that turned into a habit. On the days I scheduled a workout, I made that workout my top priority. I knew I would be too tired and lazy to hit the gym once I sat down on the couch after school. And so I decided I would not give myself the chance to sit down once I got home. The second I walked through the front door, I would drop my backpack, throw on my gym clothes, and go to the gym.

I convinced myself that thirty minutes would go by quickly and even if I was too tired to push my hardest, it would still be better than doing nothing. After my workouts, I'd feel refreshed, energized, and glad I'd gone instead of sitting on the couch. To this day I still make a point to get in my workout even when I'm super tired. A workout is always worth it!

GET TO KNOW YOURSELF

So, how will you change your habits? Before you can learn healthy habits, you need to recognize your own unhealthy habits.

1. Start by making a list of all your eating and exercise rituals. Be honest with yourself and write down everything in your handy dandy journal. Do you eat fast food every day? Do you drink soda more than water? Do you get any exercise at all during the week? Do you always overeat at meal times? Do you eat any fruits and vegetables? At all?!

2. What are the choices you make that are keeping you from the body and life you want? Write down all of your bad habits here. Take some time and think about what you are doing that you know you could do better.

3. Now make another list. This time write down the habits of someone you know who is in great shape. Do you think he or she is eating a Twinkie and rotting on the couch right now? Probably not. What is he or she doing? What would you do if you were already in your best shape? Write down everything you can think of.

Whit's Tip

Hang out with your most fit friend more often or with other people you know who are fit. Watch their habits, their choices, and their energy level. You might learn why they are so fit, or at least become more motivated by being around them.

You can't think of someone you know who is in great shape? Then find someone whose body you admire and learn what their diet and fitness regime is. For example, ever wonder how Jessica Biel maintains her taut and toned physique? Well, you can be certain it is not by following the same habits you do! Look up her fitness routine in a magazine or on the web. I've read that she works out for an hour three to five times a week. She does a mix of high-intensity cardio (sprints), plyometrics, lots of core work, and weight training. And guess what? She eats healthy too, lots of vegetables and lean protein sources. She snacks on fruit and tries to avoid carbs late at night. Basically, she lives a healthy and active lifestyle.

Hmm . . . notice the difference between her habits and yours? That difference is why she looks the way she does and you are still unhappy with how you look. To get a body like Jessica Biel's you have to work at least as hard as she does. Junk food every night and sitting at the computer all day will not get you there. Now, to be realistic, Jessica Biel is a movie star with lots of money and lots of time to focus solely on looking great. You may not even want to look like her. You probably just want to lose enough weight to feel good and fit in your clothes better.

The good news is you do not have to follow her diet and exercise routine exactly to get results. Right now you're a beginner, and doing anything will be enough for you to start changing. What you should learn from Jessica is her healthy lifestyle habits: regular exercise, healthy diet, self-discipline, and consistency. It's about time you adopted these kinds of habits.

When you read your lists, which one makes you feel better about yourself? Snacking on junk all day or running laps around the track? Which person would you rather be? To become a new person, you have to stop being who you are now. You cannot be both. That's just the way it is. You want to change, so change. Look at your list of bad habits. How can you change these starting today? Write down what you are going to do to say good-bye to your old self and hello to the new you.

Whit's Tip

Think about your ideal version of yourself. Who would you be if you were not bogged down with insecurities about your weight? Write it down! Write down what you would look like, what kind of people you would hang out with, what kinds of activities you would do, what new things your newfound confidence would empower you to try, what you would wear, how you would speak, how you would interact with others . . . Now, write down what you have to do to become that person. Losing weight is probably the first obstacle, but is there anything else you can work on now?

Can you begin to get to know the kids in the running club your fit self would be a member of? Can you practice the flirty smile your confident self would give to that cute boy in class? Can you look online and fill a virtual shopping bag of the clothes you will wear when you've lost the weight? Think, write, and then start doing!

WEEK BY WEEK

You won't change into a whole new person overnight. You have a lot to learn yet. But you can gradually become healthy and fit by switching out one bad habit for one good habit every week. You drink soda every day? Switch to drinking water every day for the first week. Don't exercise at all? Change that by going for a walk every day for the next week. Don't eat breakfast? Make eating a healthy breakfast the next week's challenge. Get the point? Good.

Uh, not good! Drinking only water every day? Yeah, that's not happening. What about my morning sugar-loaded energy drink? Uh, too bad! If a new body is what you want, forget your old way of life and step into a better one. Suck it up and make the changes you need to. Honestly, new habits are not so hard to take up. Give it a couple weeks and they'll feel as natural to you as your old ones. Once you see the amazing results from your new lifestyle, you won't ever want to go back to your old one ever again. I sure never will!

REFORM *YOUR* HABITS

Eating breakfast every morning, choosing healthier lunch options, and sticking to my workout schedule were the three most important habits I had to adopt in order to be successful. Now it is *your* turn to switch out your bad habits with some better ones. I've already asked you to write down a list of your bad habits. Go back to that list and decide which three you think are most detrimental to your weight-loss efforts. Those are the three you will focus on changing first.

Here are some tips to help you get started:

1. Start with changing one habit at a time. Don't overwhelm yourself by jumping the gun and trying to change everything at once. Wait until you have got the hang of the first new habit before you move on to the next.

2. Set yourself up for success by preparing for success. For example, if you need to get up earlier to eat breakfast, set your alarm clock every day for fifteen minutes earlier than you normally wake up. If you need to drink more water, set a bunch of water bottles around in your kitchen, in your room, and in your backpack so you have no excuse to reach for anything else. If you need to break your habit of eating late at night, brush and floss your teeth after your last meal of the day to kill cravings.

3. Keep a chart of how many days you have successfully stuck to your new habits. Check off the days you have completed so you can see how well you're doing. It's very motivating to see how far you've come, and you'll be inspired to go even further.

4. Ask a friend or family member if they would like to join you in adopting a new healthy habit. That way you can check up on each other daily to see how well you're doing. You can even compete with each other over who can stick to the new habit the best. A little competition is healthy (heh heh heh, get it?) every once in a while!

Once you change your habits, it's only a matter of time before you see results. The trick is to give those changes enough time. Impatience only leads to frustration, which then leads to you reverting to your old ways. You will never see results if you go back to your old ways! Stick with your new habits, wait it out, and you will see that good things really do come to those who wait.

6

Diet and Exercise

Those who think they have no time for bodily exercise will sooner or later have to find time for illness.

—*Edward Stanley*

I'm going to describe a typical day in your life. I'm guessing, of course, but it's based on a lot of experience. Here goes: you wake up, eat breakfast (if you don't, you should!), then go to school. For the next seven hours you sit at a desk.

Unless you are taking PE, the only time you are not sitting is when you are walking from class to class. That's not nearly enough exercise to burn off that Twix bar you snuck from the vending machine. (Uh-huh, I saw that!) After hours of sitting and pretending to listen to what your teachers are saying, it's time to go home. You sit on a bus for another ten or so minutes until you're home. Once inside, you head straight for the pantry for a snack and then promptly crash on the couch and click on the TV. Again, you're sitting as you watch reality show reruns for another two hours or so.

Oh, can't forget homework! More sitting while you struggle with that dumb algebra equation. If you were focused, you'd complete your assignments in thirty minutes, but since you are texting your friends at the same time, it takes a bit longer.

What smells so good? Dinner! Not that you are all that hungry. Remember, you did kind of pig out when you came home from school. But your mom brought back Kentucky Fried Chicken! You have to have at least a *little bit*. That *little bit* turned into three chicken breasts, a generous helping of mashed potatoes, two biscuits, a little bit of coleslaw, and a big dollop of gravy to wash it all down. You finish dinner feeling uncomfortably full and a little guilty for eating so much.

Now that dinner and homework are behind you, it seems like you should do something. Maybe go for a walk to burn off some of that food you just ate? Eh, but you just don't feel like it. You're kind of tired after a long day at school, and the food you just ate left you feeling sluggish. Instead, you seat yourself in front of the computer and hang out on the web for the rest of the evening. Then at around 11:30 PM you finally look up from your computer screen. Wow, how did it get to be so late? You totally didn't notice time go by. Finally you get into bed so you can wake up six hours later and begin the whole routine all over again. Hmm . . . still wondering why you're fat?

THE PROBLEM

Let's revisit your daily routine. Pretty much every hour of your day is spent sitting. You sit at school. You sit at home. You don't get any regular form of exercise. In order to lose fat, you must burn more calories than you consume. Say you are a sedentary fourteen-year-old girl, you weigh about 150 pounds, and you're about five foot five. Now, let's say you eat 3000 calories in one day (the amount of calories a sedentary teen girl needs to maintain a healthy weight is only about 1600). Based on your height, weight, age, and activity level, you will burn off around 1800 calories. That leaves 1200 calories that have to go someplace. Guess where they go? Straight to fat. Yep, pretty basic concept, actually.

To gain 1 pound of fat, your body must store 3500 calories. If you are consuming 3000 calories (or more) on a daily basis and only burning off 1800 of those calories . . . do you see where I'm going with this? Those 1200 calories that you are storing every day would add up to a grand total of 8400 calories in one week. Did you do the math already? That's more than 2 pounds. Per week!

OK, most likely you are not gaining 2 or more pounds weekly; that scenario was just an example. Your calorie intake differs from day to day depending on what you eat. The same goes for how many calories you burn based on your activity level and personal stats (height, weight, age). Also, not all metabolisms are the same! People naturally burn more or fewer calories per minute depending on their genetics. But no matter how fast your metabolism is, if you overeat on a daily basis and do not exercise, you will continue to pack on the pounds over time.

Do you even know what 1 pound of fat looks like? Well, ever eaten a baked potato? One large baked potato weighs about 1 pound. When you gain a pound of fat, it's the equivalent of the size of one baked potato. Imagine those 3 extra pounds you're gaining every week as potatoes being stuffed inside your stomach and butt! Doesn't sound very appealing, huh? You're not a potato sack, so stop filling your body with potato-sized globs of fat!

Keep lounging around on your butt all day and you might find yourself with a whole barrel full of Idaho's finest.

The human body, your body, is designed for movement. Just think about how the human race started out. Our ancestors were all once hunters and gatherers, meaning they lived off the land and were constantly on the move in search of food. Lots of walking, lots of calorie burning. Replace hunting and gathering with fast food and TV and suddenly we've become fat.

Again, it comes down to this: most of our generation—meaning you—does not move enough during the day. If you aren't moving, you're not burning any extra calories, and extra calories are converted into fat. It is one of the body's basic survival instincts. You see, your body tries its hardest to keep you alive no matter how badly you treat it. When you overeat, your body takes those calories and stores them as fat for backup energy. Your body does not know when it will next be fed. For all it knows, it could be days or weeks before you eat again.

To save you from dying of starvation, your body will then use the extra fat it stored (in your belly and thighs and butt and, well, you get the idea) as energy if needed. Every time you move, that fat is being burned as fuel. The problem with so many of us today is that we do not move enough to burn off the fat we have stored.

Whit's Tip

Get some exercise in now! Jump in place ten times, then run in place for ten seconds, then do ten jumping jacks! Do you feel a little out of breath? Do you feel your heart pumping? Good! Those are signs you are not only burning calories but conditioning your body to be healthier! Just that little bit you did made a difference. What if you did even more?

After a while, all that extra fat takes a toll on your body. Fat weighs down your limbs, making it harder for you to move quickly. Fat puts more pressure on your bones and ligaments. Ever notice how after standing or walking, your feet and back start to hurt? This is normal for everyone, but the heavier you are, the more quickly your bones will fatigue. So much additional weight is too much for your body to handle.

Worst of all, extra fat puts more pressure on your heart. The more you weigh, the harder your heart must work to pump blood throughout your body. A human heart can only handle so much pressure before it gives out.

THE ONGOING PROBLEM

Go on for too long feeding your body unhealthy foods and not exercising, and one day your body may stop working altogether. Yep, years and years of eating crappy foods laden with fat and sugar has a definite adverse effect after a while.

You are more at risk for developing cancer, diabetes, and heart disease. This also means you're at greater risk of dying earlier. Think I'm being overly dramatic? Then consider this fact. People are having heart attacks younger and younger. How many more years will it take before we see ten-year-old children going into cardiac arrest? Not long, I'm sure, unless something changes, and soon.

It has taken our parents' generation decades of living an unhealthy lifestyle to build up enough gunk in their hearts and arteries to have major health problems and weight issues—yet it only took me fourteen!

I remember being around eleven or twelve years old and going to the doctor for a checkup. They wanted to take a blood sample and check my blood pressure. The nurse had trouble taking my blood because my arms were carrying so much extra fat it was hard for her to find my veins. Then when she tried getting my blood pressure, the child-sized armband wouldn't fit around my arm. She had to leave and find an adult-sized armband. *That* was embarrassing. I felt like I must be the only kid who couldn't use the *kid* size because I was too fat for it. I was barely a preteen and already big enough to be considered adult size. Today I'm sure this is an all too common problem for a lot of kids. But oversize arms aren't the only issue becoming too common.

Heart problems, diabetes, and cancer are no longer only associated with "old people." Nowadays it's not unusual to hear of a young person dealing with one of these maladies. Childhood obesity is a huge health risk. A study done by Dr. Geetha Raghuveer of The Children's Mercy Hospital in Kansas City found that obese children as young as ten had the arteries of an average forty-five-year-old adult! Elementary school kids should not have arteries as thick as a middle-aged adult. Clogged arteries can cause life-threatening heart attacks and strokes. Seriously, this is no joke. If you keep on filling your arteries with grease and fat, it won't be a question of *if* you'll die of a heart attack. It will be a question of *when*.

How long do you think it will take for you to develop one of these problems? Do you want to have a heart attack? Do you want to get diabetes? Do you want to grow so fat that visiting Disney World would mean you'd need a motorized wheelchair to get you from ride to ride?

I know you know what I'm talking about. You've seen those severely obese people at amusement parks trailing slowly behind their family in one of those motorized scooter-type things. Those people have allowed themselves to get so big that just standing in line for too long is a challenge. A lot of them cannot even fit in the seats on the park's rides!

And then there are the stories of men and women who ate themselves to the point where they could not even leave their homes. They became so obese that their bodies could not handle the stress of walking from their bedroom to the front door. In some cases they became too big to fit through the front door. Imagine that. Imagine a life where you are immobilized by your own fat, confined to your bed, with nothing to do but eat more and more.

Don't take this lightly. If you continue with your current lifestyle, who is to say you won't end up the same way? Consider this: those bedridden, obese people started out normal, just like you. They put on the weight over the years by eating too much and exercising too little—*same as you*. Do you need a crystal ball to see yourself in, say, ten to fifteen years?

Now, really, how embarrassing and terrible would it be for you to die from overeating? "Yep, she just kept shoveling it down until one day her body gave out midbite." You don't want that to happen to you. I don't want that to happen to you. And it won't happen to you, not if you get off your butt and do something about it!

THE SOLUTION

Fortunately, there is hope. Nothing in life is permanent—unless you allow it to be. You don't have to remain fat. You don't have to keep getting fatter. You can change if you really want to. It is not your destiny to be overweight throughout life. You made yourself fat and now you will make yourself fit.

Whit's Tip

If you are able to get to a gym, perfect! If you can't, or you prefer to work out at home, that's OK too! Right now scout out some good places to exercise. Maybe there are some places outside that would work? Look for a staircase you can run up and down, a grassy area where you can drop down and do sit-ups and push-ups, or a trail you can jog on. It could be in your house too. A corner of your room, the basement, living room, garage . . . The more you plan ahead of time, the easier it will be to jump right into a fitness routine.

Exercise is essential for your well-being. Without exercise your body grows sluggish and you begin to feel tired much of the time. With exercise your body becomes leaner and more limber and you feel more energetic throughout the day.

When I first started exercising, it was not easy. Exercise was definitely not my favorite activity, let me tell you. I had gone for so long being ridiculed for my unathleticism in PE and on the playground that just the thought of working out made me uncomfortable. I was so worried about what people would think of me. Like, "What is this girl doing in the gym? She's so fat! She's only kidding herself if she thinks walking on the treadmill is gonna do anything for her." Yes, I was *that* self-conscious.

My self-consciousness was part of the reason it took me so long to finally get moving. Every time I felt motivated to get up, I quickly sat back down when I thought about how trying to exercise would give people yet another reason to make fun of me. See? Another way in which my weight held me back. A stupid reason. I shouldn't have been so ashamed of myself to do something that was good for me. It was ridiculous, but I didn't see it that way then.

When I realized I was never going to change unless I did something about it, I told myself to suck it up. I was going to have to just do it whether people made fun of me or not. I didn't want to live the rest of my life afraid of what people would think.

That first week was hard. Every day I went to the gym in my apartment complex and walked on the treadmill or walked outside for thirty minutes. My gym was tiny, containing only two treadmills and a few weight machines. Luckily, I had the place to myself most of the time since it was summer vacation and I could go during the day when most people worked. Sometimes, though, other people would be in the gym, or come in while I was working out, which always made me feel uncomfortable. I would worry about what they were thinking of me. "Wow, she's big. I guess it's a good thing she's here" or "Ha ha, look at that fatty huffing and puffing on the treadmill."

Of course, it is unlikely anyone was actually thinking such thoughts but in my mind they were. I had to learn to get past my silly anxieties. And I did. After a week or two, I got used to exercising every day and I found I didn't worry so much what others might or might not be thinking about me. I became comfortable at the gym—it became *my* gym. Most important, I was enjoying the walking and even sweating! It made me feel . . . healthy!

Whit's Tip

Just *have* to watch your favorite TV show every day? Then make that half hour count by getting in some movement. Instead of sitting and watching, stand up in front of the TV and march in place! During commercials get on the floor and do sit-ups or push-ups or maybe even some stretching. As soon as your show comes back on, hop up and march away!

Two to three weeks later, school started up again. Ninth grade, my first year of high school. By that time I had already lost 10 pounds! I was ecstatic! My friends and classmates could see a difference and were surprised at what I had done. I was surprised too, and more motivated than ever to keep going.

Those 10 pounds melted off with me only walking at about a 3.7-miles-per-hour pace every day for thirty minutes. My diet hadn't even really changed yet; I was still eating a lot of crap. It occurred to me that if I could lose 10 pounds with that small level of effort, I could probably lose a whole lot more if I worked harder!

I kept going for my walks. Each time I pushed myself a little more. On the treadmill, I tried walking faster or changed the incline from 0 to 1 then 1.5, 2, 2.5. During my walks outside, I pushed myself to go just a bit farther every time. All this walking was making me feel great! And the weight kept dropping right off!

My ultimate goal was to become a runner. Running had always been difficult for me. I told myself and everyone else that I hated running but secretly I loved it. I wanted to be able to run for miles, but at 230 pounds I could run for maybe thirty seconds! I guess I had a love/hate relationship with running. I loved it because it was what I wanted to be able to do, and I hated running because I wanted to do it so badly and couldn't. It was a real source of frustration.

But now it was time for me to run. I knew this was what I wanted to do. I also knew running would shed a lot more weight than walking. Minute by minute, I built up to jogging for thirty continuous minutes. It didn't happen overnight, oh no. I had never run for longer than a minute or two at a time in my life! Progress was slow. Eventually I would alternate from running (at a slow pace!) for a minute to walking a few minutes, then running again. Each time I would try to run longer than I had the day before. Seven months and many pounds later, I could run a full thirty minutes without stopping. That's way longer than thirty seconds!

Running was becoming a passion, but my workouts didn't stop with the treadmill. Daily I would scour fitness magazines and search the internet for different exercise routines—thank goodness I love to read! My dad had a set of dumbbell weights, rarely used at the time. I moved them into my bedroom, where I would perform the workouts I'd found. During my search for new moves, I learned a lot about health and fitness. I learned about how the body burns calories. I learned what exercises burned the most calories and which built the most muscle. I learned about how important a healthy diet and regular exercise are to losing weight.

Through my new knowledge, enthusiasm, and actions, I continued dropping pounds. I felt unstoppable. My weight was dropping so fast; it was incredible!

PEAKS AND PLATEAUS

I definitely felt on top of the world—or my own private mountain peak—when my weight was dropping so fast. But life can't be spent entirely on a mountain peak, and weight doesn't keep dropping at an almost unbelievable rate. Working out was new and challenging for me at first. But I got stuck in a routine that eventually became too comfortable. Yes, I continued working out and improving my diet, but that was it. I continued doing the *same* thing at the *same* level of effort. This definitely worked for a while but it couldn't work forever. With about thirty pounds left to go, I had hit my first plateau.

Fit Chick Chats

naraB: Hello Whitney!!! I was SOOO inspired by ur story!!! I'm overweight and I read ur story and I was inspired to do something about it THIS summer!!! So I'm following the 6-week plan and I hope I can lose weight! U really inspired me!! Thank u!! And could u please give me some tips about eating and exercise . . . that's if u have time thanks!!

WH: Hi naraB! Yes, go for it! School-free summer is the perfect time to get on track with a workout and healthy diet routine. The best diet advice I can give you for just starting out is to be aware of what you are eating at every meal. Are you eating mostly food that comes out of packages? Are they fried foods? Sugary foods? Greasy foods? If they are, make a point to switch out those foods for lighter options. Choose steamed over fried and go for fruit when craving something sweet. The less processed your food is, the better.

The human body is a pro at adapting to whatever conditions are forced upon it. If your body is used to eating the same amount of calories and getting the same amount of exercise, you will stay at the same weight. However, start feeding your body fewer calories and exercising more and your body will adapt by burning fat, until it reaches the point where your calories in = calories out.

I was doing great at keeping up with regular exercise, and my diet was better, though not nearly as good as it could have been. The problem was that I had stopped progressing in my effort level and was doing the same thing at the same effort for the same amount of time. I was also not making any more changes to my diet, eating the same amount of calories. Well, after doing the same thing for too long, my body adapted to these conditions. It no longer needed to burn extra fat because what I was doing was just enough to sustain my current weight.

When this happened, I didn't understand I had hit a plateau. All I knew was that I was working out and nothing was happening! That would not do. I hadn't come so far only to stop before I had reached my goal. Here is where, yet again, my love of reading paid off. I did my research and learned about plateaus and, most importantly, how to overcome them. Either work out harder or eat better. I decided I should do both.

And I did. I made more of an effort to eat healthier, staying away from fast food and sweets. I went to the gym and ran harder, inching my speed up to running thirty minutes at five miles an hour to six miles an hour. These changes forced my body to adapt again, and again I was losing weight. The key, I discovered, to seeing results is your effort level. Whenever you feel you can go a little bit longer or push a little bit harder, do it. Continue to challenge yourself and you will make amazing changes to your body.

CALCULATE YOUR BMI

I know you are anxious to reach your goal weight, but do you have any idea what that is? Your goal weight should be based on what is healthy for your personal body type. Maybe you've heard of it and maybe you haven't, but the BMI (body mass index) scale determines the recommended weight for your height. Basically, it assigns a number to your specific height and weight measurements. To figure your BMI:

1. Weigh yourself. Write that number down (be honest!).

2. Measure your height in inches. Write that number down too.

3. Figure your height squared.

4. Divide your weight by the number from step #3.

5. Multiply by 703.

A BMI below 18.5 is considered underweight, between 18.5 and 24.9 is in the normal range, 25 to 29.9 is overweight, and 30 or more is considered obese. The BMI chart is not necessarily 100 percent accurate since it doesn't take into account muscle mass or gender. But it does give you a general idea of where you are in terms of health.

Here is an example of what *my* BMI was when I was fourteen:

Weight = 230, Height= 5'7" (67 inches)
BMI calculation: [230/(67)^2] x 703 = 36

You can also check online for BMI calculators that will do the work for you. Some calculators do take into account gender and age and will give you a more accurate estimation. If you feel like you're not as healthy as you should be, check your BMI to see where you fall on the chart.

Check out what my BMI is now:

Weight = 130, Height =5'8" (68 inches)
BMI calculation: [130/(68)^2] x 703 = 19.7

Remember that how healthy you are really depends on how you feel. When you know you are eating healthy, exercising regularly, and feel and look great, then you don't have to pay attention to the number on the scale. But if you've been eating too much fast food, don't exercise at least a few days a week, and often feel sluggish or sick, these are signs you're *not* healthy. Knowing your BMI is a good start to getting on the healthy track. Your goal is to get within the healthy range for your stats. Recalculate your BMI every week to see where you are. As progress begins to show in the mirror, the numbers will show it too!

7

Get Started

The secret of getting ahead is getting started.

—*Mark Twain*

Well, now you know why exercise is so important—not only for the sake of skinny jeans, but for your life! OK, so you've just been given a lot of information, and no doubt it's all a bit overwhelming. Don't worry; soon you'll be a fitness pro! But remember, being healthy and fit is a *lifestyle*, not something you should do occasionally. You're not going to look great in a bikini all year round if you work out only every so often.

FITNESS PLAN

So first things first: make a fitness plan. Think about your daily routine. Where in your life do you have time to get in a workout? Is it in the morning before you go to school? Is it right when you come home from school? Or is it after dinner?

Think about where you are and what you are doing at every part of the day. To be successful it is important you set up a realistic workout schedule around the events of your everyday life. You will be more likely to stay with a routine if it is already a planned part of your day.

Fit Chick Chats

scanter223: I'm a sophomore and I don't even want to look at the scale to see what my weight is but I'm sure it's around 230. I want to look better and feel better about myself but I just don't know where to start or what to do to change. I really want to do something. I just need the guidance to get started on what I should do. Like what should I eat every day and what kind of workouts should I do?

WH: Hi scanter223! I know how you feel (obviously) and I'm proud of you for making the decision to change your life for the better. The best way to start is by being aware of everything you can do right now as a beginner. If you are getting little to no exercise everyday, make a point to move more. Go for a walk, do jumping jacks during TV commercials, or play a sport with your friends. Get in some form of activity everyday. You should also be making better decisions at your mealtimes. If you have a choice between the fried chicken or the grilled chicken, choose the grilled chicken. If you have a choice between the banana split sundae or a fruit salad, choose the fruit salad. It's the everyday choices you make that will change your body.

And please do not make the excuse of not having any more room in your schedule to fit in a workout. You *do* have time—you just have to make it. If you truly are busy with after-school activities or whatever, maybe it's time you lighten your load a bit. Your health should be your main priority. Ask yourself this question: what is more important to you right now—being involved with twenty different clubs at school or getting the healthy body and confidence you've always wanted, *for life*? The choice is up to you; just make sure you make the right choice. And don't expect not to make some sacrifices.

Whit's Tip

Are you generally more motivated when working in a group setting? Then sign up for a fitness class! Most gyms offer tons of different exercise classes to choose from, so you're bound to find something you like. Even if you do not belong to a gym, they will sometimes allow you to take their classes for a small fee. Local community centers sometimes offer fairly inexpensive fitness classes as well. But if paying to work out is just not in your budget, then get to a computer and look up free fitness classes in your area. You might get lucky and find something close by. If not, maybe there is a sport, walking, or running club at school you would be interested in joining. Or maybe your church offers free dance or aerobics classes? Find out now and sign up before you have time to talk yourself out of it!

FITNESS JOURNAL

Once you have thought about the best time for you to exercise, write it down in your journal. For the sake of organization, you might want to use a separate notebook (or a computer if you're tech savvy) to record your workouts. Whatever you decide to use, keeping a fitness journal will allow you to plan and track your workout progress. Most all fitness professionals keep a fitness journal—me too!—because it is important to stay on top of your workouts and fitness goals.

On a blank page, start by writing the days of the week, Monday through Sunday. Decide which days you will exercise on (it's best to shoot for three days a week!). Beside each of your workout days, write down what type of exercise you plan to do and for how long. Chapters 8 and 9 detail lots of exercises for you, but for now just start with what you already know how to do. Can you walk for thirty minutes on Monday, jump rope for ten minutes and then bike for twenty on Wednesday, and dance to your favorite ten songs in your room on Friday? This is your workout plan for your first week.

Monday
30 minute run ✓
20 minutes weight lifting ✓

Tuesday
Boxing class ✓

Wednesday
Rest ✓

Thursday
Cycling class X
* 40 minute run ✓

Friday
30 minutes weight lifting ✓
* 15 minutes on elliptical ✓

Saturday
Boxing Class ✓

Whit's Tip

Lay out your workout gear the night before. When it's time to work out, you won't waste any time (or have any extra time to rethink about exercising) rummaging through your closet for something to wear. You can don your shorts and sneakers and get right to it! Plus, seeing your workout gear lying around somewhere in your room will be a reminder to stick to your new healthy lifestyle.

In the following pages of your journal, make an entry for each day of the week. Every day, record your exercise (if it is a day you had not planned on working out, then write that in as your rest day) and whether or not you stuck to your workout plan. Also, write down any extra notes about how your workout went. Did you work out as long as you planned? How did you feel before and after you worked out? Was this workout easier or harder than the day before? Did you push yourself as hard as you could have? And so on. These notes will be helpful when you plan future workouts.

Every week start this process over. Create your workout plan for the week and then track your progress daily. Most fitness experts agree that you need to work out at least three days per week to see significant results in body composition. Did you get that? You must work out at least three days per week, every week! This is completely different from working out three days in one week and then not working out again for another month. You won't be seeing results any time soon if that's your idea of a fitness regime. Regular exercise must become a part of your life.

I know this might sound time consuming. After all, you still have to get your homework done, right? But, honestly, keeping a fitness journal won't take you more than ten minutes a day, total. Just ten minutes! Besides, don't you think the extra time is worth it if it means the difference between you getting a rocking body or not?

When I began keeping a fitness journal, it completely changed my attitude toward working out. I went from doing my best to squeeze in a workout three days a week to making fitness my top priority. I started to see myself as an athlete, not just someone who got on the treadmill to burn calories.

My level of fitness dramatically increased after I began fitness journaling during the last few months of my weight loss. At that time, I worked out for thirty minutes three days a week. It was tremendous progress from when I first began my weight-loss journey, but I wanted to improve even more. My idea of fit was being able to rub shoulders with the athletes at my school, even though I couldn't serve a volleyball if my life depended on it! Keeping a fitness journal allowed me to get to that level.

Whit's Tip

Need more motivation to get you going? Join an online weight-loss support group! There are other teens out there going through the same struggle with weight that you are. A support group will allow you to share your progress, setbacks, and struggles and receive encouragement from other teen girls just like you. Getting started takes a lot of effort, but it will be so much easier knowing you've got others cheering you on.

By tracking my workouts, I could see how much progress I was making week after week. When I noticed areas where I could improve in my workout (by working out longer, pushing a bit harder, or trying a new routine), I would note it in my journal and work on that area the next time I hit the gym. The results were that I gradually got fitter. My strength increased, my endurance increased, and my body composition improved.

My thirty-minute workouts three days a week turned into forty-five-minute workouts four to five days a week. I loved to work out and couldn't imagine skipping a workout for anything! It was great being able to look back in my journal and see the progress I'd made. I used to be the girl who nearly had panic attacks at the thought of going to gym class. Now I was in better shape than my gym teachers!

A fitness journal is a definite *must* if you plan on rubbing shoulders with the athletes at *your* school. Or if you just want to look like you could (after all, not all of us are born with volleyball-serving abilities!). Anything you can do to keep your mind focused on fitness is a huge help in determining your weight-loss success.

EVERYDAY FITNESS

Don't think the only time you need to be active is when you're in a gym. Having a fitness mind-set means you make fitness part of your everyday life. There are plenty of ways to stay moving that don't involve treadmills or fancy exercise machines. Here is a list of things you can do every day to keep your body moving!

* Walk to and from school (if possible) instead of taking the bus.
* Speed walk between classes at school.
* Offer to be your teacher's helper when he or she asks for an assistant to run errands, hand out papers, clean the chalkboard, and so on.
* Take your dog out for walks more often.
* Help out around the house: fold the laundry, mow the lawn, take the trash out, mop the floors . . .
* Always use stairs instead of elevators and escalators. Always!
* Ditch the remote and get up every time to turn the TV on or off.

* Play games with your siblings: hopscotch, kickball, jump rope, tag . . .

* Push the grocery cart during your trip to the grocery store (this works better if your cart is really full).

* Park as far away from your destination (store, mall, school) as you can.

* Don't hang out with your friends sitting on the couch in your basement. Instead, walk around the neighborhood while you guys catch up on school gossip.

Your daily activities can help aid in your weight loss if you make a little extra effort. Get used to being active! Banish any excuse you might have for being lazy and turn it into an opportunity to burn some extra calories. There is always a more active solution to every one of your routine activities (except for maybe sleeping).

EXERCISE BASICS

When it *is* time for you to be in the gym, there are a few basics you need to learn before starting an exercise program. First things first: check with your doctor before you begin any fitness routine, especially when you are new to strenuous activity. You want to make sure your body is capable of performing certain exercises without resulting in serious injury. Ask your doctor if there are any forms of exercise you should avoid until you get in better shape. You'll also want to make sure your doctor checks your heart, blood pressure, lungs, and any other vitals that could affect your physical fitness. When you know you're in the clear, the next thing you need to do is throw on some comfy clothing. It's really hard to get your body into certain positions if you're wearing tight-fitting or nonelastic clothing. A plain T-shirt and sweatpants or elastic-waist shorts will do. You might want to consider a sports bra too. Bras are not the most comfortable thing to jump around in. And make sure you've got some comfy shoes on as well. Boots, flip flops, or high heels will not work at all. They can actually be dangerous if they cause you to trip up while you're exercising, so don't wear them! Any kind of tennis, running, or walking shoes will be just fine.

Once you get that out of the way, it's time to warm up! You can sometimes do your body more harm than good if you work out without warming up first. Before you jump into a hard workout, you need to make sure your muscles and joints are loose enough to handle the work. A warm-up should be anywhere between five to ten minutes long. During that time you should be doing easy movements that warm up your muscles and get your blood flowing. A brisk walk or slow jog, light stretching, or simple calisthenics (such as arm circles, knee raises, marching in place) are all good ways to get your body ready for a harder workout. You should do a similar routine at the end of your workout to cool down. Stretching out your muscles at the end of a workout will help prevent soreness and strain while increasing mobility.

Also, remember that if at any time during your workout you feel intense pain anywhere in your body, it's best to discontinue the workout and go straight to cool-down. You should never feel completely comfortable during exercise (duh! It's meant to be work!). Sweating, fatigue, and muscle soreness are all normal during and after a workout. You will most definitely feel discomfort if you have never worked out much before. But don't worry; these are signs that you are challenging your body to grow stronger. However, it is possible to push your body too hard. If at any time you feel lightheaded, dizzy, queasy, or breathless (It is normal to be out of breath when working your body hard, but you should not feel like you are suffocating), or you experience joint pain during a workout, stop.

Take a few minutes to catch your breath and wait for the symptoms to subside before you resume your workout. If these symptoms do not subside within five minutes of stopping, go straight to cool-down and call it a day. This is a likely sign that you have overworked your body, and in that case, you need to take it easy next time or take a day off altogether. It's just as important that you let your body recover from exercise as it is that you exercise.

If you are experiencing severe pain or it is difficult for you to move a certain body part in certain ways, you should see a doctor. This might mean you have sprained a muscle or hurt it in some other way. To heal properly it will most likely need a cast or sling and lots of rest. But don't worry! Usually, these kinds of injuries heal pretty nicely and you should be good to go after it's healed.

Now that we have got all *that* out of the way, it's time to begin an exercise program! Learning anything new can be challenging at times, so don't be discouraged if you have to start slowly. Seriously, there is nothing wrong with being completely horrible at an exercise if you have never done it before. The important thing is that you still attempt to do it, even if you can't do it perfectly. Remember, slow and steady wins the race! Now get out there and win!

8

Get Moving

Physical fitness is not only one of the most important keys to a healthy body; it is the basis of dynamic and creative intellectual activity.

—*John F. Kennedy*

Let's get our fitness on! Warming up was easy. Now it's time to get down to business: fat-burning business, that is. Get ready to sweat, because that is what a fat-burning cardio workout is all about! I'm sure you've heard of cardio exercise before, but do you know exactly what it is and what it does for you? No? Don't worry—that's why I wrote this book! I wouldn't ask you if I wasn't going to explain it to you.

CARDIO FOR EVERYONE

Cardio, short for cardiovascular, is any form of movement that gets your heart pumping and your blood moving. Walking, running, swimming, and playing sports are all forms of cardio exercise. Not only does cardio burn a lot of calories, but it improves your fitness in other ways as well. Regular cardio exercise will decrease blood pressure, improve blood circulation throughout your body, increase your muscle and cardiovascular endurance, decrease stress, improve your mood, increase energy, raise your metabolism, and, of course, decrease body fat. Basically, cardio exercise gives you a healthy heart and healthy lungs, which are the foundation of your body's wellness.

Now, there are two types of cardio: low intensity and high intensity. Low-intensity cardio is any kind of exercise you can perform at a somewhat comfortable pace that doesn't skyrocket your heart rate. You shouldn't be so out of breath that you could not carry on a conversation with someone if you had to. A brisk thirty-minute walk, a thirty-minute jog, an hour-long bike ride—these are low-intensity cardio, because you are moving at a moderate pace. You are able to complete the exercise over a long period of time because you are pacing yourself.

Whit's Tip

While we're talking about cardio, why not get up and start walking while you read? I am serious! It's not so hard to read while you pace back and forth—unless you are incredibly uncoordinated. In that case, just stand while you read! It burns more calories than sitting and reading, right?

High-intensity cardio is any kind of exercise that you can only do in short bursts, typically thirty to sixty seconds. When you are doing a high-intensity cardio workout, you are giving it your all; therefore, you can only do it for a short period of time. Sprinting is a great example of a high-intensity workout. When you run sprints, the idea is to run as fast as you can. But it is literally impossible for someone to sprint longer than a few minutes. It's too tiring. Have you ever heard of anyone sprinting a marathon? That is why high-intensity exercise must be done in short bursts with short rests in between. Otherwise, you'll run yourself into the ground!

Both forms of cardio are good for you and both are effective for fat loss. The difference between them is this: while both low-intensity and high-intensity forms burn calories and fat, high-intensity exercise burns more calories and fat in a shorter amount of time. For example, a twenty-minute sprinting workout can burn the same number of calories as forty minutes of jogging. Why is this so? Because with high-intensity workouts, you are exerting more force and more effort. Your body has to work harder, and the harder you work, the more fat you burn. So, you're probably thinking, "Well, great! I'm going to do only high-intensity cardio because it burns more calories in less time." Remember, though, high-intensity workouts require a lot more effort and are a lot harder than low intensity ones. To do high-intensity cardio every day would be too hard on your body, especially if you are not used to exercising. This is why you should combine both kinds of cardio in your workout routine. It is also important to do both so that your body and your muscles do not get too used to one type of movement. The more you change routines, the more calories your body will burn, trying to adjust.

CARDIO FOR BEGINNERS

When I was losing weight, I didn't know much about working out. What I did know was that I had to do something and I had to do that something consistently. That's why I began walking—at least I knew how to do that! And it worked! But that was just a start. I eventually worked up to running instead of walking, which led to faster weight loss and a drastic improvement in my cardiovascular endurance. I went from the girl who could barely run half the length of a straightaway on the school track to running 26.2 miles in one day!

Pretty cool, right? You can do the same thing! Well, if you want to run a marathon, that is. Running 26.2 miles in one day is kind of crazy and not for everyone (unless you are as crazy as I am!). The good news is that you do not need to run a marathon to improve your cardiovascular endurance. Thirty minutes of cardio a few times a week is good enough to start. In that thirty minutes you could:

Go for a walk: Turn your typical walk around the block into something more invigorating. Look out for stairs, hills, logs to cross over, or other obstacles to get more of a calorie burn and keep things interesting. If you're near a beach, walk in the sand. It's a bit more challenging than pavement, which means you will burn more calories!

Hike: Hiking along scenic mountain trails is not only a beautiful way to spend half an hour—it's also a great way to burn fat! Carrying a backpack loaded with supplies makes it even more of a workout.

Swim laps: Swim back and forth in the pool and see how many laps you can complete in those thirty minutes. Take it as a personal challenge. Can you do six laps? How about seven? Maybe eight and a half?

Stair climb: Climb the steps of the bleachers in your school football field (or any public stairs or bleachers). How many times can you climb up and down the entire set of bleachers before time's up?

Bike around town: Biking is an excellent exercise for your leg muscles. And it's fun! Go for a ride around your neighborhood or wherever you feel like it, and enjoy. For added intensity, turn your gears up.

Dancing queen: Admit it. We all have wished we had the moves of our favorite pop artists in their latest music videos. So why not learn them for yourself? Find a dance tutorial on the internet and break it down until you've got those moves down pat. Or just turn on the radio and come up with your own moves!

Hit the park: Play some extreme Frisbee with a friend (your dog works too; just make sure your dog doesn't do *all* the running!), kick around a soccer ball, or even play on the jungle gym!

Walk the dog: If you don't have your own dog, why not walk someone else's? You can even turn dog walking into a part-time job. You'll get paid to work out! What's better than that?

Split it up: Split up your workout by doing three different exercises in ten-minute intervals. For example, try ten minutes of jogging, ten minutes of bike riding, and then ten minutes of dancing. Pick any kind of exercise in any order you want!

Whit's Tip

Think you need to be outside or in a gym to do cardio? You're wrong. All you have to do is just start moving. Do anything you want! Dance, jog in place, skip around your room, jump up and down on your bed (if your parents catch you, you didn't hear it from me!), put on your favorite music and pretend you're a rock star performing at a concert (not that *I've* ever done this before). Do this for fifteen minutes and you'll see why you don't need anything but your body to do an effective workout.

This is all I want you to focus on for the first month. Aim to get in at least thirty minutes of low-intensity cardio three times a week. If you can do it more than three times a week, great! Low-intensity cardio does not put much strain on your muscles and therefore is safe to do more often (but only if your body agrees!). I want you to get used to the idea of exercise in your everyday life. After one month you will feel and maybe even see the difference that regular exercise makes to your health and appearance—even something as simple as walking.

CARDIO POWER

High-intensity cardio is no walk in the park, literally. There will be no mention of dog walking (unless you're walking an Italian greyhound racing dog) or peaceful bike rides. High intensity means, well, high intensity! You won't have time to smell the roses during one of these workouts. Your mind and body must be fully focused on what you're doing. But don't let that scare you into thinking these workouts will be too difficult to even attempt. Remember, high-intensity cardio is intense, but only for a very short amount of time. It will be over before you know it. So go on and give it a try!

In the following pages, you'll see specific directions for various exercises. I got into the nitty-gritty because I want you to have a solid guide to go by. But remember, if any workout in this book is more intense than you bargained for, don't get frustrated and quit. It is OK if you cannot do the workout exactly as written. Do still complete the workout but kick it down a notch. Cut the workout time in half or take longer rest breaks. If it feels too easy, crank it up!

To help give you ideas for various levels of intensity, I've added suggestions for different levels of fitness experience (beginner, intermediate, advanced). You might start by following the main instructions and then decide to lower the intensity by following the intermediate- or beginner-level variations. Or after doing an exercise a couple times, you might decide you're ready to kick it up to the advanced level! Listen to your body and adjust the level of your workout if it feels either too challenging or not challenging enough.

Intervals

Beginner: Moderate intervals are 2 minutes; hard intervals are only 30 seconds.

Intermediate: Moderate intervals are 2 minutes; hard intervals are 1 minute.

Advanced: Moderate intervals are 1 minute; hard intervals are 1 minute, 30 seconds.

If you have been working out for a while now and think you want to take your cardio to the next level, you might be ready for cardio interval training, where you will shift between intervals of low- and high-intensity cardio during the workout.

1. First, pick your cardio exercise of choice (for example, walking, running, or cycling) and start off with an easy 5-minute warm-up.

2. At minute 5 pick up your pace a little, just enough that you could carry on a conversation if you had to, but not easily.

3. Continue this pace for about 2 minutes.

4. Now it starts to get hard. At minute 7 increase your speed or your effort to nearly as hard as you can for 30 to 60 seconds. For example, if you are walking, walk as fast as you can or break into a jog for 30 to 60 seconds.

5. Then slow back down to your usual carry-on-a-conversation pace.

6. Stay at this pace for 1 to 2 minutes before speeding up again for another 30 to 60 seconds.

7. Continue this pattern until you have done at least 5 to 8 bouts of high-intensity intervals.

8. Finish off with 5 minutes at an easy but brisk pace.

The entire workout should look something like this:

Minutes	Intensity Level
0–5 (warm up)	Easy (walk in the park)
5–7	Moderate (a brisk—like you have somewhere to be—pace)
7–8	Hard (as fast as you can go!)
8–9	Moderate
9–10	Hard
10–11	Moderate
11-12	Hard
12–13	Moderate
13–14	Hard
14–15	Moderate
15–16	Hard
16–17	Moderate
17–18	Hard
18–20	Moderate
20–25 (cool down)	Easy

On Your Mark, Get Set, Go!

Beginner: Instead of sprinting straightaways, speed walk.

Intermediate: Add to your rest by walking partway back around the curve before you sprint the next straightaway.

Advanced: Jog the curves instead of walking.

Like racing? Neither do I, but sprinting is high-intensity cardio like no other. Use your school's track for this workout if you can. If you're competitive and actually do like to race, bring a friend along so you can run against each other; you might find it more motivating when you have a purpose for sprinting like a track star. Here is how to do the workout:

1. Warm up by walking or jogging two 2 laps around the track.

2. Begin at the start of a straightaway (the straight sections of the track) and sprint (this is where your racing partner comes in handy) the entire length (100 meters).

3. After sprinting a straightaway, catch your breath by walking around the curve on the track. When the curve ends, your rest ends and it is back to sprinting the straightaway.

4. Continue this cycle until you have completed at least 6 straightaway sprints (3 full laps).

5. Cool down by walking or slowly jogging 2 laps around the track.

If you can't get to a track, you can still do this workout. Go for a walk outside. When you are warmed up a bit, pick a spot about 100 meters in front of you (the length of ten school buses lined up front to back) and sprint as fast as you can until you reach that spot. Slow back down to a walk and catch your breath for a minute. Then pick another sprinting point. Repeat at least 6 times.

Jump Rope

Beginner: Aim for 15 jumps (or only as many as you can do).

Intermediate: Aim for 30 jumps; rest 60 seconds.

Advanced: Aim for 45 jumps; rest for 45 seconds.

Jumping rope is harder than it looks (try it and you'll find out). Besides being a great calorie burn, jumping rope is also a great leg, butt, and shoulder toner. Make sure the jump rope you use is the right length for your height. To determine the correct length for you, stand on the middle of your jump rope with one or two feet. If the handlebars reach your armpits, you're good. If they come up above or below, you need a different rope.

1. Warm up with 5 minutes of jumping jacks, marching in place, or stretching.

2. Turn on some upbeat music and start jumping rope. Aim to do at least 30 jumps (one jump = each time your feet hit the ground) before taking a 30- to 60-second rest.

3. Continue this cycle for a full 15 minutes. You will be so sweaty after this workout that you'll literally feel the fat melting off your body.

Whit's Tip

Use everyday objects to help you get in a workout when you're stuck at home. For example, low sturdy chairs or step stools are great for doing step-ups. Step up on the chair or stool and then carefully step back down. Repeat at least 10 times (or as many times as you want!), alternating between your left and right legs.

KEEP YOUR WORKOUTS INTERESTING!

Doing the same workout routine over and over is not only monotonous and uninteresting; it can also lose effectiveness. Your muscles respond better when they are challenged and introduced to new movements. Plus, when you have some variety, you will be more likely to have fun while working out and more motivated to stick to your workouts. Doing something new or switching things up every once in a while will keep you looking forward to your gym time.

Machine Hop

Sticking to one machine at the gym for 30 to 60 minutes straight can get boring. Try machine hopping. Maybe do 10 minutes on the treadmill, then 10 minutes on the stationary bike, and finish with 10 minutes on the elliptical. Your workout won't feel as monotonous and you'll work different muscle groups at each machine. The more muscle groups you work, the more effective your workout will be.

Pop in a DVD!

Nowadays you can find pretty much every kind of exercise video you can think of online or at the video store or library. I often followed along with workout videos while I was losing weight. I still do now! It's like going to a fitness class in your own living room. Plus having someone scream at you from the TV to push harder can be really motivating.

Exercise Your Brain

If you don't already read fitness and health magazines, start now. Fitness magazines feature new exercise plans every month. Go to the store or library and pick one up sometime. You'll find a bunch of fitness advice and workout ideas. I'm always skimming through magazines looking for new workouts to try.

Learn Something New!

Taking a fitness class is a great way to learn a new skill, have fun, and get in a great workout. If you belong to a gym, chances are they offer a variety of different classes. Boxing, kickboxing, and cycling are a few of my favorites.

Climb Stairs

You know how you get winded from walking up just one flight of stairs? That's because walking up stairs is exercise! Find a flight of stairs at home or near where you live. Walk or run up and down them 10 times. Your quads should be burning by the time you finish. You'll burn a lot of calories and strengthen your legs at the same time.

Play!

You don't have to be a kid to play games, especially games that are great for burning fat, like tennis or volleyball. When you play you're having fun and don't realize what you are doing is exercise. If you and your friends need something to do, suggest some kind of game. Everybody likes tag!

9

Get Strong

Strength does not come from physical capacity.
It comes from an indomitable will.

—*Mahatma Gandhi*

I'm assuming you want a tight, toned body and not a skinny but flabby kind of body. Well, if that's your goal, you have got to build muscle. Did you know that when you lose weight you're not just losing fat—you're losing muscle too? Losing muscle is not a particularly good thing. Not only will it make your body weaker and more prone to injuries, but it will also make your body loose and soft. Muscle tone gives your body that tight look and feel. Picture celebrities like Jessica Biel, Heidi Klum, or Halle Berry. You think they just naturally have those lean, gorgeous curves? Nope. They all use strength training (along with their cardio routine) to get that awesome muscle tone. Don't believe me? Look it up for yourself! Google the workout routines of some of your favorite celebrities and you will find bicep curls and squats galore. Trust me on this, not even celebrities can get a great butt without doing a single squat.

MUSCLE UP!

If you add strength training into your diet and exercise program, you will maintain muscle mass and build muscle at the same time, all while you lose weight. It's like the best of both worlds, really. *Oh, well, that's not such a big deal, you might think. I just want to be skinny, not muscular, so I don't care if I lose muscle or not.* Oh, trust me: you will care when you have lost a lot of weight and are left with a soft and jiggly skinny body. And don't think that lifting weights or doing too many push-ups will give you big man-muscles. It won't. Remember the celebrities I mentioned before? They've got muscle, and none of them look manly in any way. The only way you are getting muscles that big is if you weight train for years (or take steroids—and those will make you sound like a man too!).

Depending on how active you have been up to this point, you may or may not have much muscle. Muscle takes a while to build, and you won't see the physical difference right away. Muscle lies beneath your layers of fat, and in order to visibly see results, you must lose enough fat. But guess what. Muscle burns fat! Yep, the more muscle you have, the more calories you burn throughout the day. Why is this so? Muscle takes more energy to maintain than fat does, so your body works harder to keep it there. Even while you are lounging around doing absolutely zilch, your muscles are burning calories! So what does fat burn while you're sitting still? Um,

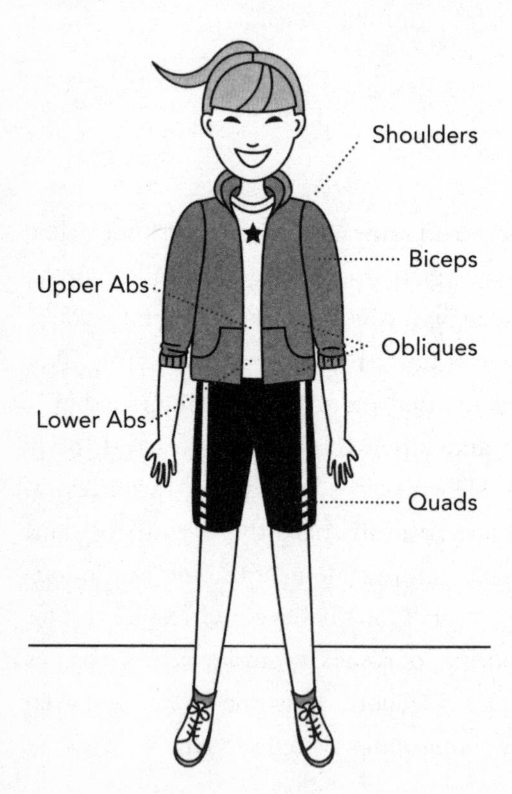

pretty much nothing. Basically, the more muscle you have, the less fat you will have. Start pumping some iron and doing those push-ups, and in a few weeks you will feel yourself getting stronger. The stronger you are, the easier your workouts will be and the better you will look and feel.

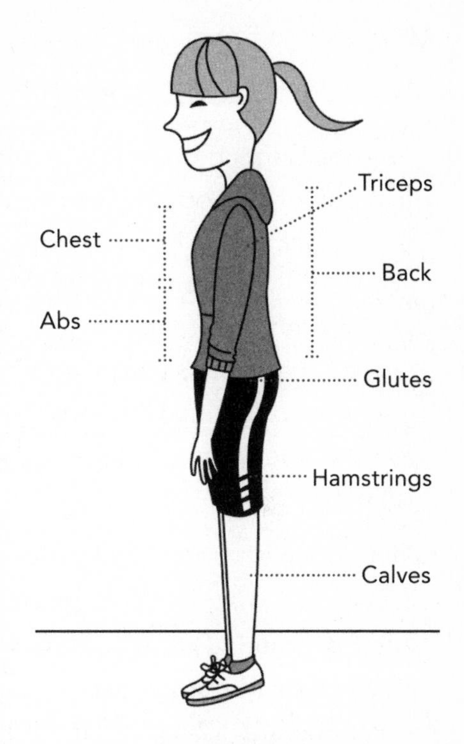

I made a list of some very basic yet effective workout moves you might want to try when you're ready. Remember that at some point you must do some form of resistance training to get a tight, toned body! A lot of these moves may require a set of dumbbells. Dumbbells are weights that have a short bar connecting two round metal balls or discs. They come in a variety of weights (you might want to stick to the three- to ten-pound range if this is your first time working with dumbbells) and can be bought pretty much anywhere. Check a sports store or a retail store such as Walmart or Target if you're interested in buying some. If you can't get your hands on any, use substitutes: soup cans, gallon milk jugs, water bottles (you can fill these with sand and/or small rocks to make them heavier), or even a sturdy bag filled with heavy objects (perfect for biceps curls!).

And just in case you're not familiar with the terminology, I'd better explain what reps and sets are. *Rep* is short for repetition. It is used to describe the number of times you repeat a complete movement of a certain exercise. So if someone said you must do sit-ups for 12 reps, that would mean you would do 12 sit-ups. You do reps one after the other; there is no rest between each rep. And when an exercise requires you to work one side of your body at a time, repeating the exercise on both sides equals one rep (unless, of course, the directions tell you otherwise).

Whit's Tip

Feel the burn now! Don't wait until you go to the gym or buy your first pair of dumbbells. You can work out anytime, anywhere! Try it now. Pick up the heaviest object in the room (but not too heavy! You need to be able to safely lift it by yourself) and hold it while you do ten squats (page 97). Did you feel that in your thighs? Good! That means you're working those muscles and already on your way to getting killer legs! Now, take that object and perform ten shoulder presses (page 93). Are you feeling it yet? No? Then do more!

A set is a continuous number of completed reps you do. After each set you take a small rest in order to gain your strength back to do another set. For example, 12 reps of sit-ups is one set. If someone told you to do 12 reps of sit-ups for 3 sets, this would mean you would do a total of 36 sit-ups, with short rests between each set of 12.

Below are descriptions of different weight-training and body weight–resistance exercises. Read over the directions and study the pictures carefully to ensure you do the moves correctly. The better your form the more effective these exercises will be.

For a full workout, pick five moves from any list of exercises (you can mix body-weight, dumbbell, and plyometric moves if you want). Each time you do this workout, try switching up the moves to work different muscles.

WEIGHT-TRAINING EXERCISES

For these exercises, you'll need some dumbbells (or dumbbell substitutes). Use a weight that you can safely lift over your head. Just make sure it's not so light that these moves aren't challenging.

Shoulder Press

Works: Shoulder and triceps muscles

Beginner: 3- to 5-pound weights, 3 sets of 10 reps

Intermediate: 5- to 8-pound weights, 3 sets of 10 reps

Advanced: 8- to 10-pound weights, 3 sets of 10 to 12 reps

1. Stand with your feet shoulder width apart. Holding a dumbbell in each hand, lift your arms to your sides and bend your elbows, bringing your weights up to shoulder level with your palms facing forward.

2. From here, carefully extend your arms upright so the weights are above your head and your arms are straight.

3. Lower the weights back to shoulder level.

Going all the way up and back down to your shoulders equals 1 rep.

Chest Press

Works: Chest, shoulder, and triceps muscles

Beginner: 5- to 8-pound weights, 3 sets of 10 reps

Intermediate: 8- to 10-pound weights, 3 sets of 10 reps

Advanced: 10- to 12-pound weights, 3 sets of 10 to 12 reps

1. Lying on your back on either the floor or an exercise bench, hold a dumbbell in each hand and bring your weights down nearly to chest level, or until the backs of your arms touch the floor.

2. Your palms should be facing forward as you lift both dumbbells straight above your chest.

3. Bring the weights back down to chest level.

Going all the way up and back down to chest level equals 1 rep.

Biceps Curl

Works: Biceps muscles

Beginner: 3- to 5-pound weights, 3 sets of 10 reps

Intermediate: 5- to 8-pound weights, 3 sets of 10 reps

Advanced: 8- to 10-pound weights, 3 sets of 10 to 12 reps

1. Stand with your feet shoulder width apart while holding a dumbbell in each hand.

2. With your palms facing up, bend your right elbow and lift the dumbbell in your right hand up to your shoulder. Only your forearm should be moving. Your elbow and shoulder stay put.

3. Bring your arm back down to the starting position and repeat with your left arm.

Two curls (one on each arm) equals 1 rep.

Triceps Extension

Works: Triceps muscle

Beginner: 3- to 5-pound weights, 3 sets of 10 reps

Intermediate: 5- to 8-pound weights, 3 sets of 10 reps

Advanced: 8- to 10-pound weights, 3 sets of 10 to 12 reps

1. Stand with your feet shoulder width apart. With both your hands, hold one lightweight dumbbell above your head.

2. Lift the dumbbell over and behind your head.

3. Slowly lower the dumbbell until it touches your upper back, right between your shoulder blades.

4. Bring the dumbbell back up over your head.

Completing steps 1-4 equals 1 rep.

BODY-WEIGHT EXERCISES

For these moves the only equipment you'll need is you! Your own body weight provides plenty of resistance to build muscle. If done the right way, of course. Again, make sure you carefully read over the exercise descriptions before you try these moves.

Whit's Tip

If at any time a workout feels too challenging, don't get discouraged. You're a beginner; it's OK to not be perfect at first! Take it down a notch by working out for only half the suggested amount of time, or do fewer sets and reps. Also remember to do each move slowly until you get used to it. Getting the correct form down is more important than how fast you can do an exercise. Plus, you will still be working out and getting results, just at a slightly slower pace.

Squats

Works: Quad, glute, and hamstring muscles

Beginner: 3 sets of 8 to 10 reps. Take it down a notch! Use a chair for support. Sit down fully on a sturdy chair and immediately stand up.

Intermediate: 3 sets of 10 to 12 reps. Keep it steady! Squat until thighs are parallel to the floor; hold one second before returning to start position.

Advanced: 3 sets of 12 to 15 reps. Crank it up! Squat holding 5- to 10-pound dumbbells in each hand.

1. Stand with your feet flat on the floor, only slightly wider than shoulder width apart.

2. Bend your knees and lower your hips straight down, as if you were sitting on a chair. Keep your back straight, your chest lifted, and your knees in line with, or behind, your toes. You should feel your weight in your heels, not your knees or toes.

3. Squat down until your thighs are parallel to the ground, or as far as you comfortably can, hold for one second, and stand up to return to your starting position.

Together, all this equals one rep.

Lunges

Works: Quad, glute, and hamstring muscles

Beginner: 3 sets of 8 to 10 reps. Take it down a notch! Lower down only halfway during lunge.

Intermediate: 3 sets of 10 to 12 reps. Keep it steady! Lower down until thigh is parallel to the floor; hold for one second before returning to start position.

Advanced: 3 sets of 12 to 15 reps. Crank it up! Lunge holding 5- to 10-pound dumbbells in each hand.

1. Stand with your feet shoulder width apart. Keep your arms at your sides or on your hips, or you can stretch them out to both sides for balance.

2. Take one big step forward with your right foot. Keeping your back straight, bend your front knee to lower yourself toward the floor until your right thigh is parallel with the ground and your left knee is a few inches above the ground. Your right leg should make a 90-degree angle; never let your knee go past your toes.

3. Push off from your right heel as you straighten your legs and return to starting position.

4. Repeat with other leg.

Completing steps 1-4 equals 1 rep.

One-Leg Dead Lifts

Works: Hamstring and glute muscles

Beginner: 3 sets of 8 to 10 reps. Take it down a notch! Instead of raising your back leg in the air every time you bend down, rest your leg behind you on a sturdy elevated surface (like a chair) and keep it there while you perform the entire movement. This will make balancing on your other leg a lot easier!

Intermediate: 3 sets of 10 to 12 reps. Keep it steady! Perform the exercise as written, but bend the front knee slightly.

Advanced: 3 sets of 12 to 15 reps. Crank it up! Perform the exercise as written while holding 5- to 8-pound dumbbells in each hand.

You know the spongy-looking stuff on your butt and the back of your legs (if you don't know what I'm talking about, lucky you!), also known as cellulite? Do this move enough, and it will go bye-bye!

1. Stand with your feet shoulder width apart.

2. Extend your left leg behind you so that your toes are lightly touching the floor.

3. Shift your weight to your left leg and slowly bend from the waist, reaching both hands toward the floor while your right leg rises behind you. Try to keep your back and your left leg as straight as possible during the entire movement.

4. Bend down as far as you comfortably can and then slowly rise up to your starting position.

One dead lift on each leg equals 1 rep.

Push-Ups

Works: Arms, chest, back, abs

Beginner: 3 sets of 8 to 10 reps. Take it down a notch! Perform the push-up vertically against a wall as you would on the floor. Stand a few feet away from the wall and place both hands shoulder width apart on the wall in front of you, arms straight. Bend your elbows as you would for a normal push-up and lower your chest as far as you can toward the wall. From here, push up, returning to start position.

Intermediate: 3 sets of 10 to 12 reps. Keep it steady! Perform the push-up as written, but use the modified plank position as described in step 1.

Advanced: 3 sets of 12 to 15 reps. Crank it up! Perform the push-up as written, pausing for one second at the bottom of the movement.

1. Start in plank position (with your hands shoulder width apart on the floor, your arms straight and elbows locked, your back and pelvis straight and parallel to the floor, your feet together on the floor, your knees locked, and your toes curled under). Or start in modified plank position, with your knees on the ground but everything else the same.

2. Bend your elbows, bringing your chest as close to the floor as you can without actually touching the ground. Remember to keep your back straight and your butt down, but not sagging. Try not to let your stomach touch the floor or your butt rise in the air.

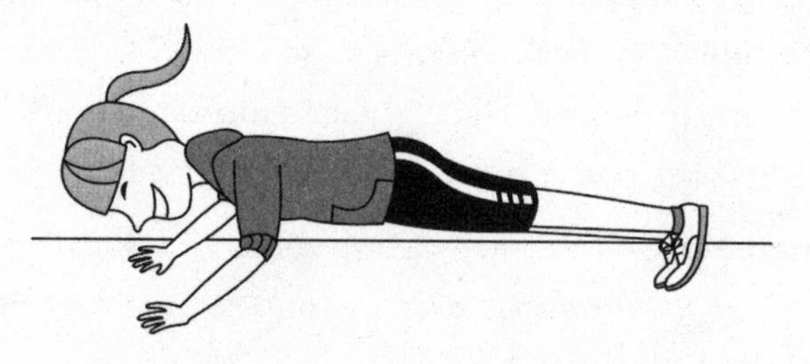

3. From here, push up through your hands, straightening your arms until your elbows lock and you are back to your starting position.

This equals 1 rep.

Triceps Dips

Works: Triceps muscles

Beginner: 3 sets of 8 to 10 reps. Take it down a notch! Keep both feet planted flat on the ground in front of you. Lower your body only as far as is comfortable.

Intermediate: 3 sets of 10 to 12 reps. Keep it steady! Perform the exercise as written, pausing for one second at the bottom of the movement.

Advanced: 3 sets of 12 to 15 reps. Crank it up! Perform the exercise as written, but alternate lifting one leg slightly above the ground during the down movement.

For this exercise you will need a chair, a bench, or some kind of stable elevated surface. Make sure whatever you are using is sturdy and intact. You will be using it to support your body weight and if your object isn't capable of doing so, it's a problem! Save yourself an injury by making *sure* your object is strong enough to handle your weight.

1. Sit on the edge of the seat and place the heels of your hands next to you.

2. Keeping your hands where they are, scoot off the seat and straighten your legs out in front of you, your heels on the floor.

3. Bending only your elbows, lower your body straight down until your elbows make a 90-degree angle.

4. Push through the heels of your hands, lifting your body and straightening your arms until you return to your start position.

This equals 1 rep.

Whit's Tip

Try this now. Lie on the ground flat on your stomach, arms by your side or straight out in front of you. Now push yourself back up into standing position. Not incredibly hard, was it? You have probably done that a million times before. But did you realize you were using almost every part of your body to do that? Try lying down and standing up ten to fifteen times in a row. You might start to notice then just how much you use your body to do even the simplest of movements.

AB EXERCISES

Your core muscles are used for pretty much every physical activity you do throughout the day (such as walking, running, bending down), as well as any form of exercise. The stronger your stomach muscles are, the better you can perform any kind of physical activity. Strengthening your stomach muscles also increases your stability and balance, which comes in handy when you are learning a bunch of new workout moves!

However, to get these benefits you must make sure you perform ab exercises correctly. Otherwise you could end up straining your neck or back. When doing any kind of ab exercise, make sure to keep your spine and neck as straight as possible. And when using your hands to support your neck during a movement, make sure you do not pull on your neck. Your hands are there for light support, not to aid in lifting your torso off the ground. When you have gotten the correct form down, you are ready to begin working on your abs.

Sit-Ups

Works: Upper and lower abs, obliques

Beginner: 3 sets of 8 to 10 reps

Intermediate: 3 sets of 10 to 12 reps

Advanced: 3 sets of 12 to 15 reps

1. Start by lying on your back flat on the floor with your knees bent and your feet on the ground.

2. Lightly fold your arms across your chest with your hands resting on each shoulder, or place your hands behind your neck, interlocking your fingers together.

3. From this position, raise your torso off the ground until your chest meets your knees. Make sure your feet are firmly planted on the

ground during the whole movement and that your back and neck are as straight as possible.

4. Lower your torso back down to the floor in starting position.

This entire movement equals 1 rep.

Crunches

Works: Upper abs

Beginner: 3 sets of 8 to 10 reps

Intermediate: 3 sets of 10 to 12 reps

Advanced: 3 sets of 12 to 15 reps

1. Start by lying with your back flat on the floor with your knees bent and feet on the ground.

2. Put both hands behind your neck and, keeping your chin away from your chest, raise your shoulders and upper back off the floor.

3. Come up halfway to your knees, and then lower down.

Completing steps 1-3 equals 1 rep.

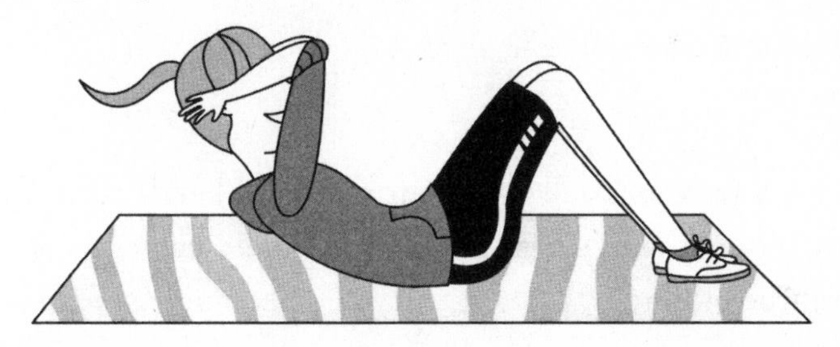

Fit Chick Chats

Latinchica14: Hi Whitney! My name is Natalie and I am 15 years old turning 16 in May, and I really want to look good for my birthday. I weigh about 148 now and I would like to weigh 125 but I can't seem to get there fast enough. Can you please help me and give me some advice and workouts to help me reach my goal faster?

WH: Hi Natalie! It sounds like you are in a rush to lose weight. Sometimes having a deadline works well for you in that it gives you an extra bit of motivation. However, sometimes it can make you so anxious that if results don't come within a few days you get frustrated and give up. My advice would be to forget about losing a certain amount of weight in a certain amount of time. Don't worry about how long it will take you, just focus on getting there. Stick to a healthy diet and get as many workouts in as you can throughout the week. The weight will come off in its own time.

Reverse Crunches

Works: Lower abs

Beginner: 3 sets of 8 to 10 reps

Intermediate: 3 sets of 10 to 12 reps

Advanced: 3 sets of 12 to 15 reps

1. Lie down on your back with your arms and hands palm-side down on the floor at your sides. Your knees should be bent and your feet flat on the ground.

2. Bring your knees toward your chest and lift your hips up. Slowly lower your feet and hips until your feet hover only an inch or so off the ground.

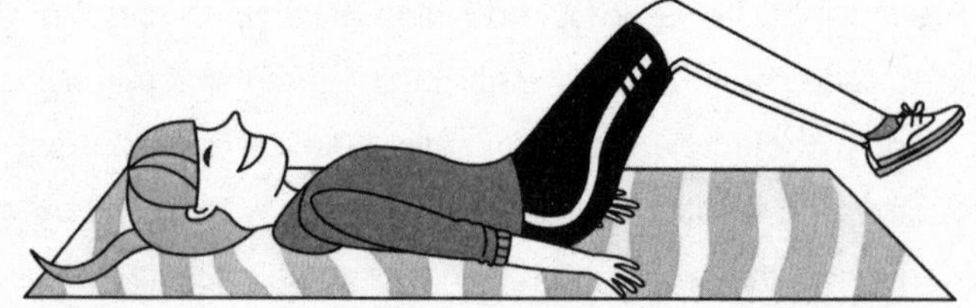

This counts as 1 rep. From this position, repeat for suggested number of reps.

Obliques Crunch

Works: Obliques (aka the area on your sides where love handles like to grow)

Beginner: 3 sets of 8 to 10 reps. Take it down a notch! Keep your legs bent during this exercise if straightening them feels too challenging.

Intermediate: 3 sets of 10 to 12 reps

Advanced: 3 sets of 12 to 15 reps

1. Lie down on your right side with one leg on top of the other. Keep your legs as straight as possible.

2. Your right shoulder should be on the ground as you place your right hand on your left side.

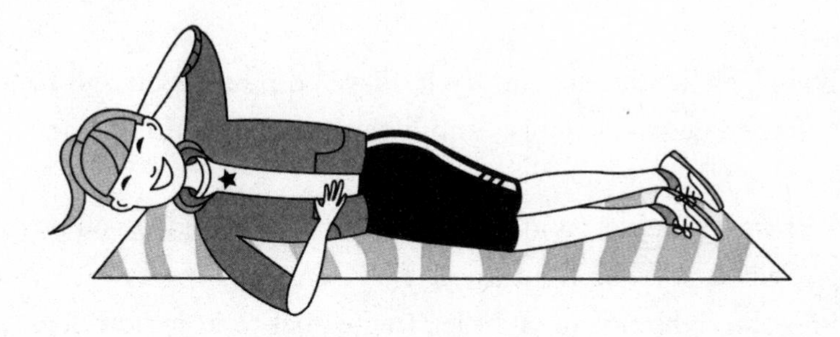

3. Keeping your legs on the floor, bring your left hand behind your head and lift toward the left up off the ground in a side crunch motion, as far as you can go.

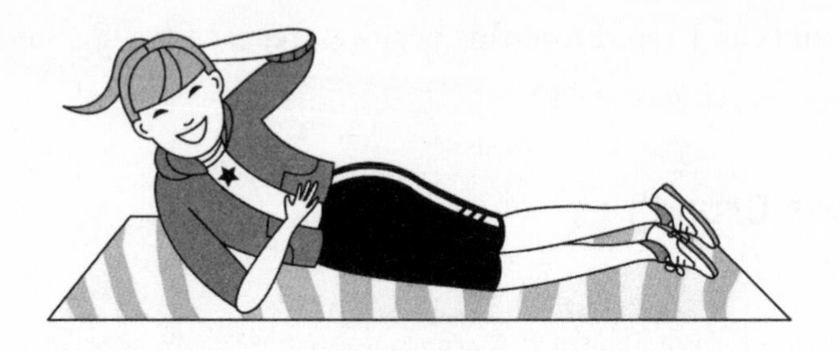

4. Then lower your body back down to start position.

This equals 1 rep.

Bicycle Crunch

Works: Obliques, upper abs, lower abs

Beginner: 3 sets of 8 to 10 reps. Take it down a notch! Keep one leg on the ground while your opposite leg is lifted toward the elbow.

Intermediate: 3 sets of 10 to 12 reps

Advanced: 3 sets of 12 to 15 reps

1. Start by lying flat on your back. Place both hands behind your neck and then bend your knees and lift your legs up into the air.

2. Lift your shoulders and upper back off the ground as you bring your left elbow to your right knee. As you're reaching toward your left knee, straighten your right leg (remember to keep both legs off the ground the entire time).

3. Quickly switch sides and repeat the motion, bringing your left elbow to your right knee instead.

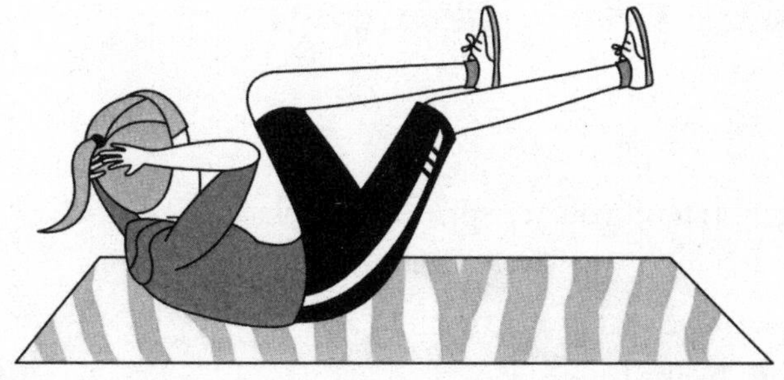

This equals 1 rep.

PLYOMETRICS

Plyometrics, in basic terms, are exercises that require you to jump. They're both cardio and power moves that are very effective for building muscle and burning calories. With plyometrics you use only your body weight for resistance. These moves are meant to be done at a fast pace for the ultimate effectiveness. If you are new to exercise, go at your own pace. Only do these moves if you think you are ready. Try completing a few reps of each exercise to see how they feel. If they are too challenging, continue with other forms of exercise until you become more fit. Wait a couple of weeks before you try these moves again.

High Knees

Works: Glutes, calves, hamstrings, abs

Beginner: 3 sets of 30-second sprints. Take it down a notch! Go at a slower pace if you have to. Instead of jumping on the balls of your feet from one foot to the next, place one foot down completely before bringing your other knee up.

Intermediate: 3 sets of 45-second sprints

Advanced: 3 sets of 60-second sprints

For this one, pretend you are sprinting in place.

1. Stand with your feet a little bit apart and your back straight.

2. Bring one knee up to your chest (or as far as you can get it up there!). Return to the starting position.

3. Next, lift the other knee. Alternate between them as quickly as you can.

4. Each time, try to land on the balls of your feet without letting your heels touch the ground.

Mountain Climbers

Works: Abs (upper and lower), upper body (chest, triceps, shoulders), lower body (glutes, quads, hamstrings), cardiovascular system

Beginner: 3 sets of 15 reps

Intermediate: 3 sets of 25 reps

Advanced: 3 sets of 35 reps

1. Start in push-up position, with your knees off the ground, your toes on the floor, and your arms straight.

2. Bring your left knee toward your chest. Put your right toe on the ground beneath your hip.

3. Extend your right leg back to where it started and set your toe on the floor.

4. Repeat with the left knee.

5. Continue to alternate quickly between knees.

Each time you bring a knee to your chest counts as 1 rep.

Jump Squats

Works: Quads, hamstrings, glutes, lower back, abs, and cardiovascular system

Beginner: 3 sets of 10 reps

Intermediate: 3 sets of 12 reps

Advanced: 3 sets of 15 reps

1. With your feet shoulder width apart, squat down as if you were doing the regular squat exercise.

2. As soon as you squat down, use your legs to jump up, getting your feet a few inches off the floor and reaching your arms toward the ceiling.

3. Once your feet hit the ground, squat down again and repeat.

One jump equals one rep.

15-MINUTE BOOT CAMP!

Get ready to blast some serious calories with this workout! You might find this one a little intense, but give it a shot. The more intense the more fat you're burning, right? Make this workout effective by going through each exercise as fast as possible.

Your goal is to see how many times you can complete this circuit in 15 minutes.

Take short breaks in between if you need to (but don't rest too long!). Once 15 minutes are up, you're done! It's a short workout, but you'll be huffing and puffing by the end—I promise.

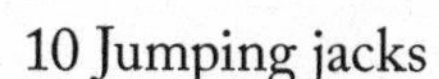

10 Jumping jacks

10 Push-ups

10 Jump squats (or regular squats)

6 One-leg dead lifts (each leg)

10 Crunches

10 Mountain climbers

10 High knees

Maybe these workouts are too challenging right now, but that's OK. You can always change the level of difficulty by trying different variations, doing fewer reps, or taking longer rest breaks in between exercises. Refer to my notes about different levels of fitness (beginner, intermediate, advanced) to get the most out of your workout.

Attempting an advanced exercise when you are a beginner will not necessarily make you stronger faster. It might lead to injury or frustration, neither of which will help you progress. Take it slow. And if doing these workouts 3 to 4 times a week is too much for your body then do them only 2 to 3 times a week. Instead do more low-intensity cardio workouts throughout the week. Just keep moving and you'll keep improving!

10

The Diet That Is Making You Fat

Don't dig your grave with
your own knife and fork.

—*English Proverb*

Do you ever think about what you eat? Do you even know what you are putting into your body? Well, sure you do. Says right there on the box that you are eating a four-cheese double-stuffed frozen pan pizza. Yum! The title is in bold letters right above the tantalizing picture of freshly baked cheesy perfection. You can almost smell it!

There may be a blurb on the box that reads something like "Only 200 calories and 8 grams of fat." Hmm . . . is that so? What you probably don't notice (you're too busy drooling over the mouth-watering picture) is the nutritional information printed on the side of the box in itty-bitty letters.

CALORIES

Look closely, read carefully, and learn. Ah, the 200 calories and 8 grams of fat are *per serving*. Big difference. Suppose one serving is one slice, or one-twelfth of the pizza. Were you to eat the entire pizza (which you easily could) you'd have consumed 2400 calories and 96 grams of fat! Whew! That's more than enough calories to get you through an entire day! Even if you ate only half of the reheated slab of cheesy dough, you'd still be consuming 1200 calories and 48 grams of fat. That is *way* too many calories and fat for one meal.

According the 2010 USDA dietary guidelines, the average number of calories a moderately active teen girl needs daily in order to maintain a healthy weight is 1600 to 2000. Total fat intake for a teen girl should be no more than 25 to 35 percent of her total calories per day (and they should be healthy fats! I'll explain later). Based on a 2000-calorie diet, that means only about 56 to 78 grams of fat per day. Hmm . . . did you just take a moment to look back at the stats of your beloved frozen pizza? Now do you understand why even eating half of that thing is contributing to your inability to lose weight?

Whit's Tip

Throw out all the junk food in your pantry and fridge!!! Can't throw it out because your family won't let you? Fine. Then push all of the junk food to the back. Hide it behind healthier foods so that the next time you open your fridge or pantry you're reminded of healthier options. You might even forget you have that bag of potato chips in the pantry! Instead you'll reach for an apple, or you might decide you weren't even really hungry to begin with and walk away with nothing. Either way you're saving calories and doing yourself a favor.

INGREDIENTS

As if that weren't bad enough, the nutritional value of all those calories and fat is pretty much zilch. Take a look at the ingredients list for a frozen pizza. What you will find is mainly white flour, cheese, and sugar. Oh, and let's not forget all the added chemicals that preserve, enhance, and colorize the pizza. "Huh? What chemicals?" you ask. Read the ingredients. You'll find a list of additives you probably can't pronounce and likely have never heard of. And you thought maybe they were exotic spices or something, right? Ha!

Nope, your food is loaded with artificial flavors, preservatives, food dyes, and plenty of other questionable substances probably best left in chemistry class. But microwaveable pizza is not the only place you'll find them. Pretty much anything you buy that comes packaged contains some kind of unnatural additive. That's why I consider all processed foods "fake food." The amount of chemicals food manufacturers stick in their products often outweighs the amount of natural ingredients. Why would someone put chemicals in our food? Well, so you will keep buying from them, of course.

Food companies are out to sell. That means making sure their stuff tastes and looks the best. By adding various manmade chemical ingredients, they can enhance flavors, enhance color, and lengthen the shelf life of a product. *But that doesn't sound so bad*, you might think. *It just makes the food taste better.* Wrong!

Sure, the chemicals they use might enhance the flavor of your food, but keep in mind you're eating unnatural chemicals! That should really bother you. After all, you wouldn't gulp down just any funky-smelling goop someone handed to you, would you? What if you were to visit the factory where one of these chemically enhanced fake foods was produced? Suppose one of the chemists put in front of you the different additives and preservatives that go into one batch of packaged cream-filled cupcakes (there are a lot of them, so it would take up a whole table). Do you see yourself picking up each ingredient and chugging it down? I don't think so!

Sure, chemicals can be useful in our daily lives. For instance, antibacterial chemicals keep germs from spreading and people from getting sick. That's a great thing, but would you want to ingest antibacterial solution? No, because it's a chemical! Chemicals like that are not meant for you to eat. But in the end, you do. You just don't know it because they're so well hidden in that creamy, fluffy cupcake.

You should know that these chemicals can be harmful to your health. For example, MSG (monosodium glutamate) is a popular additive that is used mainly as a preservative in many convenience foods. MSG has been reported to cause headaches, nausea, weakness, breathing difficulties, drowsiness, rapid heartbeat, and chest pain in some people. Hmm . . . that's quite a lot of harmful symptoms you could potentially contract from indulging in your favorite fast foods. Do you really think it's worth it?

The bottom line is that consuming too many unnatural chemicals is bad for your health. What? Did you honestly expect to hear that ingesting chemicals is good for you? No way! And common sense would tell you that the more of them you consume, the more health problems you'll encounter down the road. You may not feel the effects now but you most certainly will when you're older.

Whit's Tip

What's the best way to avoid those sneaky chemicals in your food? Buy organic whenever possible. Organic foods are made without chemical sweeteners or harmful preservatives. They are better for you and in my opinion taste better too! Just make sure what you're buying is really organic. Foods that are made with only 70 percent organic ingredients can carry the label "made with organic ingredients," confusing you into thinking they are fully organic. Only foods that contain 95 percent organic ingredients and have been certified by the USDA can label themselves as organic. These foods will have a green and white label reading "USDA Organic." If a food does not carry this label then it is not totally organic. However, they can be pricier than nonorganic foods. If you have a tight budget right now, going all organic might not be realistic. But, hey, just do the best you can! Any healthy change you make is a good change.

Sugar

Even without the addition of risky additives, consumption of most fast foods and convenience foods poses very real health risks. What's that? Fast food can't be *that* bad, you say? Well, what about that soda you drink with every super-sized value meal? I'm sure you know it contains a lot of sugar, but do you know what that sugar does to your body?

First of all, let me explain that there are two different kinds of sugar: naturally occurring and added. Fructose (found in fruits) and lactose (found in milk) are known as naturally occurring sugars because they occur naturally in foods. Added sugars are sugars and syrups that don't occur naturally in foods and instead are added to food and drinks to make them sweeter. White sugar, brown sugar, honey, and high-fructose corn syrup (HFCS) are examples of added sugar. HFCS is the worst of them all. And it's found in nearly all junk food.

Allow me to say a few words about my "favorite" fattening additive. Corn syrup is just another form of sugar, but in a very highly concentrated form. HFCS started to be used in place of natural sugar in processed foods sometime back in the 1960s because it was cheaper to produce. In 1967, about 5 percent of American teenagers were obese, according to National Health Examination Surveys. As of 2008, nearly 20 percent of middle schoolers and high schoolers were obese. Did you get that? The number of obese teens has nearly quadrupled since HFCS and other additives have started to make up a lot of our foods. It is definitely part of the diet that is making you fat.

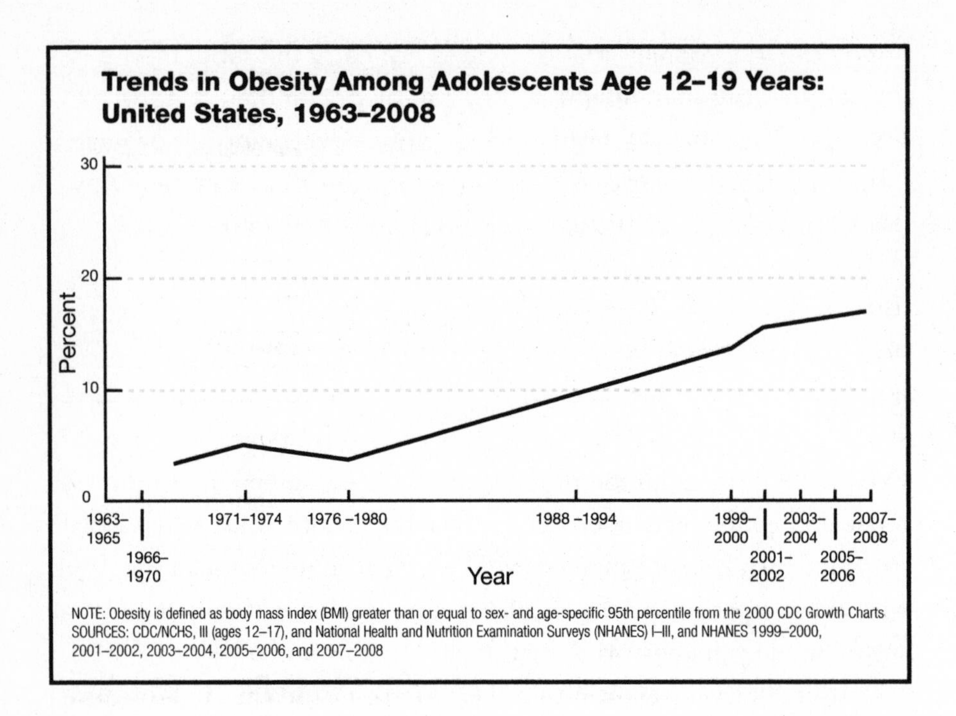

HFCS is in nearly everything we eat nowadays. Do a little research in your own fridge and pantry right now. Read the ingredients on at least three products and see for yourself. There will be HFCS in stuff you didn't even think had sugar in it, like breads, crackers, even peanut butter. While you're at it, be on the lookout for hydrogenated oils, salt, and unpronounceable chemicals. Yep, they'll be there too. If you get lucky you might find a package of cookies with every kind of additive in it: then you can get fat, clog your arteries, and develop diabetes—all from one box!

Naturally occurring sugars, however, are not necessarily a bad thing. Your body uses them for energy. The sugar goes straight to your bloodstream, where it can be readily available to power you through a quick run around the neighborhood. But if you don't go for that run, guess what? All that potential energy (sugar) is quickly stored as fat.

Eating too much sugar is also a risk factor in developing type 2 diabetes. Not only because it causes weight gain (obesity is another high risk factor for type 2 diabetes), but because too much sugar consumption over time can lead to insulin resistance. Insulin is what your pancreas produces to regulate carbohydrate and fat metabolism in your body. If you are insulin resistant, your body does not efficiently use the insulin your pancreas makes, therefore causing your blood sugar levels to rise. Then your pancreas tries to make more insulin, but your body keeps resisting it. Eventually, your pancreas tires out and just stops making insulin. That's type 2 diabetes.

Nutrition Facts

Serving Size 1 can (12 fl oz)

Amount Per Serving	
Calories 140	
	% Daily Value*
Total Fat 0g	**0%**
Sodium 45mg	**2%**
Total Carbohydrate 39g	**13%**
Sugars 39g	
Protein 0g	

CARBONATED WATER, HIGH FRUCTOSE CORN SYRUP, CARAMEL COLOR, PHOSPHORIC ACID, NATURAL FLAVORS, CAFFEINE.
CAFFEINE CONTENT: 57mg/29 fl oz

Nutrition Facts

Serving Size 1 can (12 fl oz)

Amount Per Serving	
Calories 0	
	% Daily Value*
Total Fat 0g	**0%**
Sodium 40mg	**2%**
Total Carbohydrate 0g	**0%**
Sugars 0g	
Protein 0g	

CARBONATED WATER, CARAMEL COLOR, ASPARTAME, PHOSPHORIC ACID, POTASSIUM BENZOATE (TO PROTECT TASTE), NATURAL FLAVORS, CITRIC ACID, CAFFEINE.
CAFFEINE CONTENT: 46mg/12 fl oz

Diabetes is no joke and can be life threatening. Heart disease, kidney disease, blindness, metabolic syndrome, and stroke are just some of the effects of diabetes. So what is one thing you can do to reduce your risk of developing type 2 diabetes? Consume less sugar! The American Heart Association suggests that the average woman should consume no more than six teaspoons (30 grams) of added sugar a day. Guess how many teaspoons of sugar are in one 12-ounce can of Coca-Cola? Oh, only about *seven*!

And switching to diet soda doesn't solve the problem because diet sodas are full of chemicals. You have the choice of either sugar (which will contribute to weight gain and possibly diabetes) or chemicals (which are bad, bad, bad for your health!). Which should you choose? Um, how about neither! If you want something with flavor, switch to flavored sparkling water or beverages that are sweetened with stevia (a natural sweetener that comes from plants, not chemicals).

Whit's Tip

Craving junk food? Before you dive into a box of Oreos, think about what's mainly in those cream-filled chocolate cookies. You know, fat and sugar? Now visualize what those Oreos will do to your body once you eat them. The sugar will wreak havoc on your bloodstream, spiking your insulin. The fat will have nothing better to do other than raise your (bad) cholesterol and in turn make it much more likely you'll be dealing with clogged arteries soon. Oh, and of course the extra calories will turn to fat, which you have plenty of already! Now, do you still want that box of Oreos?

Sodium

Are you starting to get why fast food is seriously bad for you? No? Well, let's move on then to the salty and greasy morsels typically found in your everyday fast food meal. The Institute of Medicine recommends adequate daily salt intake to be 1500 mg, with 2300 mg as the highest tolerable level. The average American consumes about 3400 mg of sodium per day. Sodium is found not only in those salty french fries at fast food restaurants (570 mg in a medium order of Burger King fries), but also can be found in your sodas, cheese, meat, crackers, chips, candies . . . the list goes on and on. Too much salt in your diet has been linked to high blood pressure, osteoporosis, stroke, heart disease, and even stomach cancer!

I don't know about you, but I don't think soggy, salty fries taste good enough to risk getting stomach cancer. No, thank you!

Fat

Oh, and what about all that fat that goes hand in hand with those salty fries? I already mentioned the suggested daily fat intake for a teenage girl (56 to 78 grams). Most of that fat should preferably come from healthy fats. Polyunsaturated and monounsaturated fats are needed by our bodies to function properly.

Our bodies use these fats to build cell membranes and keep our brain, lungs, eyes, immune system, and digestion process functioning well. They also help metabolize our food. These types of fats are good for you and can be found in foods such as seafood, nuts, and oils. But remember that too much of a good thing is always a bad thing. There is only so much healthy fat your body needs, and keep in mind that fatty foods (whether they are healthy or not) contain a lot of calories.

Saturated and trans fats are the bad fats. Saturated fats are found mostly in meat and dairy while trans fats (also a saturated fat) are chemically altered and are found in processed and packaged foods (check out www.heart.org for more info on healthy versus bad fats). The daily recommended amount of saturated fat for a person on a 2000 calorie diet is less than 16 grams, and trans fats, less than 2 grams.

You should know (if you haven't figured it out already!) that most fast food items are dripping with fat. To prove my point I did some research on the following fast food restaurant websites. Let me show you just how much fat (and calories) your favorite fast food contains.

No one knows how to fatten you up better than a chain restaurant! But what can this excess of fat do to your body? Consuming too much unhealthy fat raises your bad cholesterol while lowering your good cholesterol, which in turn increases your risk of heart disease and stroke. Heart disease and stroke! Hmm . . . are you noticing the pattern here? *Eating fast food causes serious health problems!* Think of it this way: every time you indulge in one of these high-calorie, high-fat meals, you are only increasing the very real risk of developing a serious health condition. And some of those conditions can potentially lead to death. Think about that for a moment. Eating unhealthily doesn't just mean you won't look good in a bathing suit. It means you might not live to even care what you look like in a bathing suit.

Restuarant	Menu Item	Calories and Fat
Burger King	1 side order of large fries	500 calories 22 grams of fat total 3.5 grams saturated fat
Chick-fil-A	Cookies & Cream Milkshake (size large)	690 calories 33 grams of fat total 16 grams saturated fat
Pizza Hut	1 personal pan cheese pizza	590 calories 24 grams of fat total 10 grams saturated fat
Olive Garden	fettuccine alfredo (dinner portion)	1220 calories 75 grams of fat total 47 grams saturated fat
McDonald's	Angus Bacon and Cheese Burger	790 calories 39 grams of fat total 17 grams saturated fat
IHOP	Breakfast Sampler	1160 calories 70 grams of fat total 21 grams saturated fat

That's why it would make sense that everyone, especially those trying to lose weight, should avoid unhealthy processed foods whenever possible. After all, everyone wants to be healthy, right? I mean, no one wants to be lying in a hospital bed. So we should all just stop eating junk food and we'll be fine . . . too bad that's easier said than done.

GOOD CHOLESTEROL VERSUS BAD CHOLESTEROL

Cholesterol is a naturally occurring substance our bodies create to help us function properly. Cholesterol is used by the body to help produce hormones, create bile that is necessary for our bodies to digest food, and act as a protective barrier for each and every one of our cells. Cholesterol cannot be dissolved into our blood. Instead it is carried to and from our cells by lipoproteins known as low-density lipoproteins (LDL) and high-density lipoproteins (HDL).

LDL is also known as bad cholesterol because when there is too much LDL cholesterol circulating around in our blood, it builds up along the walls of the arteries connected to our heart and brain. When there is too much LDL buildup in our arteries, it can form into a hard plaque that narrows our arteries and makes them less flexible. This in turn can lead to heart attacks and strokes.

HDL is known for being the good cholesterol. High levels of HDL in your bloodstream protect against heart attacks. Doctors believe this is because HDL carries cholesterol away from your arteries and back to your liver where it is disposed of by your body. They also think HDL can slow down the process of arterial buildup by removing excess cholesterol from arterial plaque.

The amount of cholesterol we have in our bodies varies by genetics and can increase or decrease depending on what we eat. Now that you know how cholesterol affects your body and which types of fats affect your cholesterol, it's up to you to make healthy choices. But this might be not be so simple.

ADDICTIONS

Whether you realize it or not, you are addicted to the salts, sugars, and fat in processed food. It's the bane of the typical American diet. Ever find yourself constantly thinking about food? When you see a bag of chips, is your body just itching to reach out and grab it? And when you do get your greedy hands on the salty devils, you can't eat just one, can you?

Face it: you're addicted to junk food. It's true. You're no better than a drug addict. People addicted to drugs lose control over themselves. They can only think about their next high. Put their choice of drug in front of them and it is nearly impossible for them to resist taking a hit. And one time won't be enough. A drug addict will keep coming back for more, until eventually *they* are no more.

Replace the drug addict with yourself and the drugs with your favorite junk food. Sounds eerily familiar, doesn't it? You are a junk food addict. If you still don't believe me, try this experiment. Imagine a handful of fresh blueberries. Now imagine a slice of blueberry pie.

Which one appeals most to you? Come on—you know it's the blueberry pie! I bet your mouth even salivated a little just thinking about it. See, I told you: you are a junk food addict.

But your addiction is not entirely your fault. The food industry will do anything to sell their products. They couldn't care less about your health and overall well-being. For them it is all about how to make more money off you. They want you to become addicted so that you'll keep buying.

Think of the food industry as the drug dealer in the world of junk food addiction. Just like a drug dealer pursues kids, hooking them while they are young, food companies target their sales toward kids. The younger you are exposed to an addictive substance, the more likely you will remain addicted and become a lifelong customer, giving them more and more money over the years. Turn on your TV and notice how many food commercials are aimed at young children and teenagers. Now go back a few pages and look again at the percentage of children and teenagers who are overweight. Notice the connection?

Sugar, fat, and salt are addicting. That is why there are huge amounts of them in all processed foods. The sweeter, saltier, and greasier something is, the more we want to keep eating it. But just as a drug addict can beat the affliction with a lot of support, self-control, and work, so can you. Reading this book is a good start. Exercising and avoiding fattening foods are great. Now read on to learn which foods are best for you. Kick that addiction to the curb!

Now do you see why you should be reading those itty-bitty letters on the back of your frozen pizza? It is your responsibility to be aware of what goes into your body. Don't mindlessly put anything into your mouth. When you do, you're acting like a two-year-old who finds a nail on the ground and tries to eat it. Stop behaving like a two-year-old! You're old enough by now to know what is good for you and to make your own food choices.

READ THE LABEL!

Get into the habit of reading the ingredients labels on all packaged and canned foods you buy.

1. First read the ingredients list so you can know what is in the food, and then decide whether or not you should be eating it.

2. Look at how much fat, sugar, salt, and calories are in each serving.

3. Note the serving size at the top of the label. You'll likely end up eating more than one serving, so be sure to multiply the fat, sugar, salt, and calories per serving by the number of servings you expect to eat.

4. Decide if this is a food that is part of a fatty diet or a healthy diet. If you choose to eat it, decide beforehand how many servings you'll eat and portion it out on a plate or in a snack bag.

5. Then put the rest of the food away so it doesn't tempt you to eat more!

Here is an example from a real bag of corn chips:

Nutrition Facts	
Serving Size 1 oz (28g/About 32 chips)	
Servings Per Container About 4.5	
Amount Per Serving	
Calories 160	Calories from Fat 90
	% Daily Value*
Total Fat 10g	**15%**
Saturated Fat 1.5g	**7%**
Trans Fat 0g	
Polyunsaturated Fat 6g	
Monounsaturated Fat 2.5g	
Cholesterol 0mg	**0%**
Sodium 160mg	**7%**
Total Carbohydrate 16g	**5%**
Dietary Fiber 1g	**5%**
Sugars 0g	
Protein 2g	

Think about eating just half a serving. But be realistic, only sixteen chips? Imagine munching on those chips while watching television. Are you going to stop after sixteen of them? *No!* More like fifty, and that's before the first commercial! Do the multiplication. Yep, that's a lot of fat and a lot of calories. In one sitting you can reach nearly half your recommended daily calorie limit by snacking on those chips. And you wonder where those bulges under your clothes came from!

11

The Diet That Will Make You Skinny

To eat is a necessity, but to eat intelligently is an art.

—François de la Rochefoucauld

So, after reading the last chapter, maybe the thought of a large order of McDonald's french fries isn't all that appealing to you right now. Am I wrong? Ha! Of course I am. Unfortunately, reading one chapter about the ill effects of fast food isn't enough to erase your cravings. But now that you know what shoveling junk into your body is doing to you, you have no excuse to continue eating it. Say bye-bye to greasy pizza, au revoir to triple-bacon deluxe Whoppers, and auf wiedersehen to Doritos Nacho Cheese tortilla chips. You won't be seeing them for a while.

Yeah, I know, saying good-bye is hard to do. But don't miss them too much; they're not worth it. Foods that make you fat are not your friends. Kick 'em to the curb and find some new food buddies. Sorry—that's just the way it's got to be. You have to change the way you eat! If you want to lose weight and keep it off permanently, there is no way around it. Come on, you didn't really pick up this book thinking I would tell you otherwise, did you? Remember, this is not a gimmicky diet book. The only information I'm giving you is stuff that actually works. Eating packaged foods laced with chemicals, doesn't work—at all.

HEALTHY VERSUS SKINNY

But what about your friend *so and so* who eats nothing but cheese puffs all day and doesn't gain a pound? Well, *so and so* may be trotting around in minuscule shorts, but that doesn't mean your cheese puff–eating friend is the picture of health. Skinny does not always equal healthy. There are plenty of people who live off junk food, do minimal amounts of exercise, and still remain thin. These people are typically blessed with small appetites and fast metabolisms that allow them to eat pizza every night for dinner without worrying about saddlebags. But while they may look great on the outside, the reality is that they are still slowly digging themselves into an early grave.

No one is immune from the ill effects of an unhealthy lifestyle. It is totally possible for a thin person to have a heart attack if they do not maintain a heart-healthy diet. It is just as possible for a thin person to be out of shape if they do minimal exercise. Next time you run into *so and so*, you might want to relay the warning. Your health should be your top priority, not just how good you look in a miniskirt.

LIFESTYLE CHANGE

I know you've heard this before, but I am going to tell you again. Losing weight is a lifestyle change. That doesn't mean eating healthy for a few weeks. It means eating healthy *forever*. This is what I mean by "the diet that will make you skinny." But don't confuse my meaning of the word "diet" with what is typically meant by the word "diet." I'm not talking about a diet where you eat only grapefruit for three weeks and are then supposed to magically drop 15 pounds. Those are fad diets. They generally are not enjoyable and they do not work. Why? They teach you what to eat for a few weeks, not for your entire life.

What I mean by "diet" is the quantity and type of nutrients you put into your body daily. Your food choices are your diet. If you are eating a crappy diet everyday, then you will not have a healthy body. If you eat a healthy diet every day, you will have a healthy body. If you eat a healthy diet for only a few weeks and return to a crappy diet, you will have a healthy body for a few weeks and return to an unhealthy body. See where I am going with this? Don't think you can change your eating habits for just long enough to lose a few pounds and then return to noshing on potato chips every night. If you do, guess what? All those pounds you lost will come back with a vengeance. Repeat this to yourself:

> **Eat like a fat person and you will be a fat person. Eat like a (healthy) skinny person and you will be a skinny person.**

Makes perfect sense, doesn't it? Keep that in mind next time you feel like taking a joy ride to Wendy's.

Eating to be skinny does not mean starvation. You don't have to live off wilted lettuce and slices of tomato to lose weight. I didn't. Definitely not. I like food way too much to eat like that! Nope, I never starved myself and yet I still shed pounds, all 100 of them. What I did do was gradually cut out "bad" foods and replace them with good foods. You could say I made new "friends," the kind who didn't make me fat. Instead of buddying up to bagels lathered with cream cheese for breakfast, I turned to multigrain toast and a healthy butter alternative. Oh, and my longtime cafeteria favorite, Mr. Steak and Cheese Sub? He was banished to the back of the menu by my lean and mean Ms. Turkey Wheat Sandwich. Sprite and Coca-Cola didn't stick around long either. Not when they had all-natural pure water to compete with. I let go of my old "friends" slowly at first, but when I saw the results my new "friends" were giving me, I gave them up more quickly.

CALORIES

And now for the question I'm sure you're anxious to ask: "Do I have to count calories?" Nope. Unless, of course, you are eating something you know you shouldn't be eating (cheese fries, for example). Calories are basically units of energy our bodies need to survive. Calories are good for us as long as we don't ingest too many of them (remember: too much of a good thing is sometimes a bad thing) or get them from the wrong sources.

Whit's Tip

Check out this site, www.wisegeek.com/what-does-200-calories-look-like.htm, to see what 200 calories looks like for different foods! Now go to your own pantry or fridge and measure out 200 calories of your favorite foods (check serving sizes to measure). Are you surprised at how little or large the quantity is for 200 calories?

To be sure you are not eating too many calories, you must consider your portion sizes. This is most important when and if—although I'd really rather you didn't do it too often—you decide to eat something (cookies, macaroni and cheese, potato chips) not deemed as supporting a healthy lifestyle. Because while a handful of potato chips won't hurt you, three, four, or five handfuls most definitely will! However, when eating healthy foods, portion sizes should be considered but there is not too much to worry about. Why? Well, a handful of raspberries won't hurt you and neither will three, four, or five.

You see, healthy calories are different from junk food calories. For instance, there is a big difference between eating 200 calories of broccoli and 200 calories of German chocolate cake. I'm assuming you can understand why that would be. Broccoli is full of nutritious vitamins and contains 0 grams of sugar and 0 grams of fat. Cake is full of . . . yeah, I think you get the point.

NUTRITION

Real foods are not only more nutritious than junk foods, they also have more bulk to them, which makes them more filling. If you ate 200 calories of broccoli, you would be extremely full. Do you know why? Because 200 calories worth of broccoli is *a lot* of broccoli, a whole plateful. Eat 200 calories of cake and guess what you get? Maybe half a small slice. Depending on what kind of cake it is, it might be only a bite or two. Really now, two bites of cake? Like that's enough to satisfy you. You know you'd have to gobble down at least two whole slices to feel even a smidgen full. In case you haven't figured it out yet, cake is not your friend.

Broccoli, on the other hand, is a very good friend. Why? Because broccoli is an example of a real food, meaning it won't add to your love handles or leave you feeling like you only had two bites of cake! Unlike the sugar-filled crap found in packages on the shelves of your local grocery store, your body metabolizes real food differently. It uses nutrients found in natural foods to restock essential vitamin and mineral stores. Therefore, your body digests your food more slowly, leaving you satisfied for hours.

That cake you ate? Well, those calories came mostly from sugar (and I've already explained what too much sugar does to you). Those calories have already traveled through your digestive system and been used up (unless you didn't work out right after ingesting them, in which case they'll be sitting in your fat cells right about now), leaving you hungry again. And it's only been an hour! No wonder you can't control your appetite. You're always hungry because you don't get the right nutrients from the crap you eat!

Do you see why your days of hanging out with Ben & Jerry must come to an end? The more time you spend with your processed buddies, the harder it will be to break away from them. To get past your junk food addiction and shed some serious weight, you've got to start eating your fruits and vegetables. Believe it or not, the more nutritious your diet becomes, the less you will crave and be tempted by foods that make you fat.

Your body will be ecstatic that you are finally giving it the nutrients it needs. It will thank you by first boosting your mood and energy. You'll be bouncing right along instead of sluggishly lumbering through the day. Next, you'll notice that your eyes shine brighter, your complexion glows, and your hair has turned silky and shiny. And then after a few short weeks of eating more "friendly" natural foods, you'll turn around and notice you've got a lot less junk in your trunk. This may all sound too good to be true but it's not. Once you stop eating like an overweight person, you'll stop looking like one.

Protein

Protein is an essential part of a healthy diet. Why? Well, we need protein to build every cell, organ, and tissue in our bodies. Because our cells, tissues, and organs are constantly rebuilding themselves, it's important we eat a steady supply of protein for this process. Protein is found in meat, fish, poultry, eggs, tofu, legumes, grains, nuts, seeds, milk, and some vegetables.

Other than being good for our bodies, protein is also good for weight loss. Protein takes longer to digest than other food groups, therefore suppressing your appetite. You will feel full and satisfied for hours after eating a high-protein meal as opposed to a high-carbohydrate meal. But don't let that make you think you should go overboard on protein shakes. Your body only needs so much protein to function properly. The recommended amount of protein for girls ages 14 to 18 is 46 grams per day. Most Americans get much more protein in their diets than is recommended.

Unfortunately, most Americans get their protein fix through animal sources in the forms of hamburgers, fatty steaks, and fried chicken. Sure, those foods are full of protein, but they are also full of calories and artery-clogging fats. It's important to get your protein from healthy sources like lean cuts of meat, baked or grilled skinless poultry, and baked or grilled fish. Milk and milk products like yogurt, raw nuts and seeds, legumes, and grains are also healthy ways to meet your protein needs as long as these sources are in their most natural state—milkshakes don't count as a healthy protein source! Basically, your protein probably is not going to be healthy if it comes from a fast food joint. Sorry!

Fiber

Did you know that fiber can help lower your risk of colon cancer, lower your "bad" cholesterol, lower your blood pressure, and oh yeah, help you lose weight? And those are just some of fiber's health benefits! Fiber is found in fruits, vegetables, and grains. It can't be absorbed or digested in our bodies. It passes through our digestive systems intact, therefore creating bulk that helps move stool and harmful carcinogens out of our bodies. Without enough fiber in your diet, you will feel sluggish and constipated: so not a great combination!

There are two kinds of fiber: soluble and insoluble. Soluble fiber is able to dissolve in water, creating a gel-like substance that helps lower cholesterol and glucose levels. Soluble fiber is found in foods like oats, rice bran, peas, citrus fruits, and apples. Insoluble fiber absorbs water, creating bulk to move food quickly through your digestive tract. This bulk is responsible for clearing away waste and toxins from your colon, therefore helping lower your risk of colon cancer. Insoluble fiber is found in foods like wheat flour, carrots, rye, brussels sprouts, and nuts.

Foods high in fiber make you feel full faster and for a longer period of time (thanks to all that bulk!), which in turn lowers appetite and can lead to weight loss. The recommended daily amount of fiber for teen girls is 26 grams. Unfortunately, most Americans do not get enough fiber in their diets. This could be part of the reason so many Americans are facing health problems brought on by poor diets. Now you know why fiber is an important part of your diet. Not just because it can help shrink your waistline, but because it could help save your life.

Carbohydrates

You've probably heard that carbs are to be avoided when it comes to weight loss. Carbs are the sneaky little devils found in breads, muffins, candy, and basically all things delicious. Yes, it is carbs that like to latch themselves onto our hips and thighs, which leads us to believe that carbs are bad. But did you know that carbohydrates are actually part of a healthy balanced diet?

Now, before you rejoice and celebrate this revelation with a platter of pancakes, know that all carbs are not created equal. The carbs that are found in foods such as pancakes, cookies, white breads, and candy are not part of a healthy balanced diet. The kinds of carbs that are good for your body include whole grain oats, whole grain breads and pastas, brown rice, green leafy vegetables, nuts, beans, and fruit.

Carbohydrates are one of the three macronutrients that your body uses for energy. Carbohydrates are broken down into glucose, which feeds your muscles and keeps your energy levels stable. The daily recommended amount of carbs for teens is 130 grams. Out of those 130 grams, most if not all should come from healthy carbohydrate sources. Remember, not all carbs are created equal!

Fruits and Vegetables

You know fruits and vegetables are good for you, but why? Well, for one thing, they are naturally low in fat and calories. Plus, they are full of fiber, which you already know keeps your digestive system healthy and your hunger satisfied. But on top of being excellent food choices for weight loss, fruits and veggies have other perks.

Many of the vitamins and minerals our bodies need come from fruits and vegetables. Potassium (helps maintain blood pressure), folic acid (used to build red blood cells), and vitamins A, C, and E (fight off infections and keep our gums, teeth, skin, and eyes healthy) are all essential nutrients we get from fruits and vegetables. It should then come as no surprise that eating more fruits and vegetables also lowers your risk of cancers, diabetes, and other diseases.

How many servings of fruit and veggies do you eat daily? I doubt it is as much as you should be eating. And no, that strawberry-filled pastry you had for breakfast does not count as a fruit serving. The daily recommended amount of fruit for teen girls is 1.5 cups, and vegetables 2.5 cups. That's per *day*.

If you are not meeting these requirements, then it's time to step it up! Start with eating an apple every day for lunch and a side of mixed veggies with dinner. Eventually, aim to eat a serving of fruit and / or vegetables with every meal. Sounds too difficult? Well, I imagine living in an unhealthy, disease-ridden body would be even more difficult. Don't you agree?

EAT THIS, NOT THAT

Have you ever heard of the *Eat This, Not That* books? They're a popular series of books that show you which of two fast food options is the "healthier" choice. I, however, have my own version of the game. But instead of helping you decide between two evils (fast food and less fattening fast food), I give you a nonprocessed natural alternative to your favorite meals.

It's actually quite simple. Instead of banana pudding, eat a banana. Instead of orange-flavored Tang, drink orange juice. Instead of potato chips, eat a baked potato. Rule of thumb: unprocessed = good, processed = bad. Basically, eat as many fruits and vegetables as you want, followed by nuts, whole grains, and lean proteins (grilled chicken, turkey, fish, and so on). Need more help? Check out this chart to find more healthy alternatives to your guilty pleasures.

INSTEAD OF THAT . . . EAT THIS!

Instead of that	Eat this
Hamburger on white bun	Veggie burger (or turkey burger) on whole wheat bun
Sweet potato pie	Sweet potato with maple syrup (no more than a tablespoon!)
Cheese-lover's double-stuffed-crust pizza	Homemade pizza on whole wheat crust with tomato sauce, skim milk cheese, and vegetables
Buttermilk pancakes topped with butter and maple syrup	Whole grain wheat pancakes topped with a small amount of syrup or honey
Greasy chicken vegetable stir-fry	Steamed chicken and vegetables seasoned with favorite seasonings
Ice cream sundae with nuts, whipped cream, and fruit toppings	Fruit salad with nuts and whipped cream topping (no more than a tablespoon or two of whipped cream)

Apple pie and vanilla ice cream	Baked apple with cinnamon and vanilla frozen yogurt
White spaghetti noodles with tomato sauce and meatballs	Whole wheat spaghetti noodles with tomato sauce and turkey meatballs (veggie meatballs work too)
Cheesy egg omelet and hash browns	Skim cheese omelet made with egg whites and cut-up baked potatoes seasoned with a teaspoon of olive oil and a pinch of salt
Strawberry milkshake	Strawberry smoothie made from skim milk and frozen or fresh strawberries
Banana cream pie	Banana with a tablespoon of whipped cream

FIGHT THE ADDICTION

I'm not saying it will be easy to change your eating habits. You've been eating wrong for so long that it seems normal to your body. Like an addict recovering from an addiction, you will struggle with cravings for junk food. The mere thought of a buttercream cupcake will have you salivating and whimpering. Getting through your school lunch line without loading your tray with fries and pizza will be a struggle. Yeah, it'll be tough, but you have to make the effort. Sometimes you've just gotta suck it up. This is one of those times.

Whit's Tip

When you feel a junk food craving coming on, shout "No!" (in your head, of course, unless you feel comfortable chastising your food cravings out loud in public). Then immediately jump into action to get your mind off those cravings! Drop down and do sit-ups or push-ups. Go for a walk. Take your homework outside where you can complete it away from the temptation of the kitchen.

HEALTHY MEAL IDEAS

All right, you get it by now. You know you must not eat processed or fast foods, but when did healthy foods ever actually taste *good?* And what about convenience? Are you realistically going to have the patience to steam vegetables for an after-school snack when that frozen burrito takes only two minutes in the microwave? Listen: healthy food does not have to taste gross and it does not have to be complicated. To prove my point I'm giving you a list of healthy meal ideas that don't taste gross and don't take long to prepare. Now you will have no excuse to reach for that frozen burrito!

Breakfast

Greek Yogurt: This stuff is amazing! By itself it tastes kind of sour, especially if you're not used to it, but add a dollop of honey and a handful of blueberries or nuts it's delicious! Also, just one cup of 0% fat Greek yogurt has 20 grams of protein and only 120 calories. With this kind of protein power, you'll be satisfied for hours. To turn yogurt into a complete breakfast try this simple recipe:

1 cup 0% fat Greek yogurt (I love Fage Total 0%)
1 tablespoon honey (maple syrup, agave syrup, fruit jelly or Stevia sweetener are other great options)
½ cup berries (raspberries, blueberries, strawberries, or any other fruit you prefer)
2 tablespoons of your favorite chopped nuts (walnuts and almonds taste great!)

Mix it all together and you've got yourself a protein packed breakfast.

Oatmeal: Oatmeal is a great way to start your day. It is warm, gooey, sweet, and surprisingly filling. For a complete fiber-filled breakfast, follow my favorite oatmeal recipe:

1 cup cooked oatmeal (or one packet of plain instant oatmeal)
1 banana, sliced
1 small handful (about 1 once) walnuts or pecans (or substitute with nuts of your choice)
1 tablespoon honey (maple syrup, agave syrup, fruit jelly or Stevia sweetener are other great options)

Sprinkle on some cinnamon and you're good to go!

Fruit Salad: I love fruit! It is by far my favorite food group. Fruit is sweet, filling, and full of vitamins. To make your own fruit salad take:

1 apple, cubed
1 banana, sliced
½ cup berries (raspberries, blueberries, strawberries, or any other in-season berries, the fresher the better!)
¼ cup grapes (red or green), sliced in half

Mix 'em all together in a bowl, and you've got yourself a fruit salad. For extra protein and fiber add a dollop of yogurt and a small handful of trail mix.

Scrambled Egg Veggie Stir-Fry: Get your skillet ready for this flavorful wake-up meal! The combination of protein (from the eggs) and fiber (from the vegetables) is guaranteed to keep you satisfied until lunchtime. Here's how to whip up this nutrient-dense meal:

2 large eggs
½ large bell pepper (or two to three mini bell peppers), sliced thinly
3 to 4 mushrooms, sliced
¼ medium sweet onion, chopped
½ cup broccoli florets
salt and pepper
tomato salsa

Using no-calorie cooking spray, stir-fry the vegetables and scramble two eggs together in a medium sized skillet, until cooked thoroughly. Sprinkle on salt and pepper to taste and a tablespoon or two of tomato salsa for more flavor.

Lunch and Dinner

Veggie Wrap: These are great for when you need to make a quick lunch. They are easy to make and easy to pack for later. Make your own lunch wrap by taking:

1 whole wheat tortilla
¾ cup of your favorite raw veggies, chopped or sliced (spinach leaves, tomato, avocado, broccoli, mushrooms, onions, pickles)

Add some slices of grilled chicken or turkey for more protein if you want. You can also add a small amount of low-fat cheese and/or low-fat dressing.

Baked Potatoes: Baked potatoes are great as part of a healthy meal. And not only are they full of nutrients, but they are filling and delicious. Plus they are super easy to cook.

1 medium russet potato
Optional healthy toppings
(Greek yogurt, salsa,
parmesan cheese,
and pepper and salt to taste)

Preheat the oven to 350 degrees. Place the potato on a baking sheet and bake for 45 minutes to 1 hour. You can also stick it in the microwave for five minutes (depending on the size of the potato, add more cooking time). Allow the potato to cool for about 5 minutes before carefully slicing along the top of potato. Top your fully cooked potato with any of the toppings mentioned. The Greek yogurt really is a delicious and healthier option over sour cream.

In my opinion, baked potatoes taste better (and are more satisfying) than french fries! Pair a baked potato with a lean protein (fish, chicken, turkey) your favorite green vegetable (such as broccoli, asparagus, or spinach) and you now have a healthy balanced meal.

Chicken Veggie Stir-Fry: Your typical chicken veggie stir-fry from your local Chinese-food restaurant is not what you should have in mind when you try this recipe. Most stir-fry recipes use huge amounts of oil or highly caloric sauces. My version is a lot lighter in calories and still tastes great! All you need is:

1 cup of your favorite vegetables, sliced, diced, or chopped (green peppers, red peppers, mushrooms, broccoli, onions, etc.)
½ cup chopped chicken (precooked chicken works best)
steamed brown rice

Using a medium-sized skillet, add a bit of non-fat cooking spray and heat the chopped vegetables over medium heat. Combine the precooked chopped chicken with the cooked vegetables and toss together. In a short time you have a delicious, healthy meal. Pair it with steamed rice for a more complete meal. But always choose brown rice over white rice. Brown rice is more nutritious and satisfying because it is less processed than white rice. Just like how I consider white bread "fluff," the same goes for white rice.

Veggie Burgers: Switching to vegetarian meat-like products not only saves the life of an animal; it saves you a lot of calories and fat. Look for vegetarian burgers in the refrigerated or frozen section of your grocery store. They come in all kinds of brands and flavors, so choose to your liking. Veggie burgers are great because they are fast and easy to make. To make a tasty veggie burger:

1 veggie burger, cooked to packaged directions
1 whole wheat hamburger bun
Add your favorite toppings (pickles, tomatoes, onions, lettuce, mustard, etc.)

Pair it with steamed veggies or vegetarian baked beans (like Bush's Best Vegetarian Baked Beans or Trader Joe's Organic Vegetarian Baked Beans), and you've got yourself a barbecue!

Snacks

Nuts and seeds: You only want to eat a handful at a time, but nuts and seeds are a must. They are good snacks because their protein and healthy fat content fill you up fast. Walnuts, almonds, pecans, sunflower seeds, pumpkin seeds, and pistachios are a few of the tasty nuts you can try.

Dried Fruit: Craving something sweet? Reach for a handful of dried fruit. Again, a handful is all you need because dried fruit is filled with sugar. When fruit is dehydrated, it shrinks because of the lost water content. Therefore, a serving of raisins will pack more calories and sugar than a serving of grapes, because there are more raisins in one serving than there are of grapes. But don't get me wrong, dried fruit is still better for you (and will most likely contain less sugar) than a bowl of ice cream. Dried blueberries, raisins, figs, dates, and (my favorite) dried bananas (different from banana chips! Check your labels before you buy) are all perfect for satisfying a sweet tooth.

Cottage Cheese: For a snack that will fill you up after a long day at school, reach for something with plenty of protein, like cottage cheese. Add a tablespoon of low-sugar fruit jam to give it a sweeter taste. The protein and healthy fat in cottage cheese will satisfy your hunger and hold you over until your next meal.

Snack or Protein Bar: OK, candy bars do not count as healthy snacks. But there is such a thing as a healthy snack that *tastes* like a candy bar! Yep, gooey protein bars and crunchy trail mix bars are so good they may taste like candy, but they are actually good for you. Their protein and fiber are the perfect way to curb your hunger during the day. Reach for one of these the next time you crave a sweet snack. But don't be reaching for them more than once or twice a day! Protein bars usually have a lot of fat and calories. While these may be fats and calories of the healthier kind, they should still be consumed in moderation. Also, keep in mind that some brands of protein and snack bars are loaded with chemicals and sugar. Always read the label. If you can't pronounce half of the ingredients on the ingredient list, it's probably not a good choice. Stick to brands with the fewest ingredients and lowest sugar content.

Hummus: Dip your favorite veggies in a couple tablespoons of hummus for a quick, nutritious snack. Hummus contains natural fats that are good for you and it even has a little bit of protein. Carrots, celery, broccoli, and bell peppers go along very nicely with this creamy chickpea paste. Forget potato chips and ranch dipping sauce! You'll feel a lot better after fresh veggies and hummus than you would after oily chips and ranch-flavored lard.

GROCERY GUIDE

Now you know how to whip up a healthy meal, and you know which foods are healthy and which aren't. But out of the hundreds of different cereal, yogurt, and juice brands, how are you to know which ones are good for you and which ones suck? Don't worry: I've got you covered. I put together a grocery guide of healthy foods and brands.

Bring this list along with you next time you go grocery shopping, or ask your parents to buy some of the foods for you. While I do advocate steering clear of processed foods, I realize it's almost impossible to do so altogether. Plus, you're just starting out. I don't expect you to go totally organic-health-freak on me yet. But some processed foods are better for you than others, like the ones I put on this list. Likewise, some brands are better for you than others. Whenever I suggest a certain brand, it's because it has less of the bad stuff than other brands I've found.

Just keep in mind that these are only a few healthy suggestions. There are plenty of other healthy foods out there that are not on this list (come on, writing down every healthy food in the world would take *forever*!). Use your own judgment, or do a little research before you buy something, to determine whether or not it will support your fitness goals.

Vegetables

Sometimes, if they're not in season, fresh fruits and vegetables can't be found in grocery stores. To give you an idea of what may or may not be in the produce section right now, I put the seasonal availability next to each vegetable on the list. Craving an out of season vegetable? No worries. Check the frozen section of your grocery store. Most likely whatever vegetable you can't find in the produce aisle will be there. Frozen vegetables are fine as long as they do not contain any additives.

* Spinach leaves/mixed greens: available year round
* Broccoli: year round
* Cauliflower: September to June
* Carrots: year round
* Potatoes: year round
* Onions: year round
* Cucumbers: June to November
* Asparagus: February to June
* Peas: April to November
* Artichokes: March to June; September to December
* Celery: April to December
* Tomatoes: June to October
* Mushrooms: year round
* Bell peppers: July to December
* Avocados: year round
* Green beans: June to November
* Sweet potatoes: September to December

Fruits

You'll notice I put seasonal availability on this list as well. If your favorite fruit is out of season, frozen or canned fruit is OK too. But be on the lookout for additives. A lot of canned fruit is packed in syrup, and frozen fruit sometimes contains added sugar. Always read nutrition labels before you buy to ensure your fruit is free of added ingredients. Dried fruit is OK to eat too and is found on store shelves year round. However, dried fruit also contains a lot of sugar, even in small quantities. It's best to eat dried fruits sparingly and in smaller amounts.

* Apples: year round
* Bananas: year round
* Oranges: year round
* Blueberries: May to August
* Raspberries: May to November
* Strawberries: March to October
* Peaches: May to October
* Melons: June to October

Dairy and Dairy Substitutes

* Low-fat, skim, or 1 percent milk
* So Delicious coconut milk (unsweetened)
* Soy milk (unsweetened)
* Rice milk (unsweetened)
* Almond milk (unsweetened)
* Zero percent (nonfat) Greek yogurt
* Low-fat plain yogurt
* Low-fat string cheese or cheese wedges
* Low-fat cottage cheese

Lean Meats and Meat Substitutes

* Skinless chicken or turkey breast
* Canned tuna (packed in water)
* Salmon
* Mahi mahi

* Shrimp
* Veggie burgers (MorningStar Farms, Boca, Amy's Kitchen)
* Veggie hot dogs
* Eggs

Bread *(look for brands that have at least 3 grams of fiber per slice)*

* Whole wheat or whole grain sandwich bread
* Whole wheat or whole grain hamburger buns
* Whole wheat or whole grain hot dog buns
* Whole wheat or whole grain tortilla wraps
* Whole wheat or whole grain mini pita bread pockets

Cereals *(check labels on cereals to be sure they do not contain HFCS!)*

* Old-fashioned oatmeal or instant oatmeal (original flavor)
* Whole grain cereal (look for cereals made from whole grains that have at least 3 grams of fiber per serving)
* Kashi GOLEAN Crunch
* Multi Grain Cheerios
* Post Grape-Nuts
* Wheat Chex
* Barbara's Bakery corn cereal
* Nature's Path cereals

Grains and Pastas

* Brown rice
* Whole wheat noodles (any type)
* Quinoa
* Whole wheat couscous

Dressings, Sauces, and Seasonings

* Tomato salsa
* Guacamole (must not exceed 50 calories per 2 tablespoons)
* Regular yellow mustard
* Hummus (must not exceed 50 calories per 2 tablespoons)
* Balsamic vinaigrette–based salad dressings

Fit Chick Chats

Madison108: Whitney, just for starters—you are such an inspiration to me. Right now, I'm 14 years old, and I'm 250 lbs. It's so hard to be called the fat girl in school. This year, I've overcome my shell, and decided that I didn't care about my appearance. I'm not sure how you were, but I'm one of the, what I would classify as, the middle group (not too popular, not too . . . you get the drift! Haha!). I was wondering since we have similar stories, if you could give me some pointers on where to start, since I am completely new to this, and have no idea where in the world to start. Thanks girl! xoxo, Madison.

WH: Hey Madison! I think it is great that you have decided to come out of your shell. Whether you realized it or not, that was your first step to becoming a healthier person. Now that you have officially decided to not let your insecurities hold you back, changing your lifestyle will be that much easier. Your next step is to decide on what results you are looking for and how to get there. Make positive healthy changes every day that will get you closer to your final result.

Nuts and seeds *(raw, not roasted and salted)*

* Pumpkin seeds
* Sunflower seeds
* Almonds
* Walnuts
* Pecans
* Cashews
* Pistachios
* Nut butters (to be used sparingly! Nut butters are very high in calories and fat)
* Peanut butter (read labels and look for a brand that does not have hydrogenated oils or HFCS. Your best bet would be to buy an organic brand if possible)
* Almond butter
* Cashew butter
* Sunflower seed butter

Snack Bars, Protein Bars, and Trail Mixes

* Nature Valley Fruit and Nut Chewy Trail Mix Bars
* Kashi Chewy Granola Bars, Trail Mix
* South Beach Cereal Bars
* Odwalla Protein Bars
* PowerBar Pria 110-calorie energy bars
* Balance Bars
* Trail mix (any brand that meets the guidelines!)
* LARABAR fruit and nut bars
* Clif Mojo Bars
* Nature's Path bars
* Any brand that does not exceed 200 calories per serving

Sweets

All right, now I know you are going to have those days where no matter how hard you try to push a junk food craving from your mind, it doesn't want to budge. Sometimes you just *need* to have something sweet or salty. While I would prefer you squash that sugar rush with a naturally sweet piece of fruit, I understand that a banana won't always do it. But instead of binging on chocolate peanut butter cookie dough cheesecake from The Cheesecake Factory, eat one of these more sensible treats. In other words, eat something that still tastes great but won't feed your already overfed fat cells. (That piece of cheesecake you wanted? 1150 calories!)

Frozen Treats

* No Sugar Added ice cream
* Frozen fruit bars
* Slow-churned frozen yogurt
* Sorbet
* Soy milk ice cream
* Coconut milk ice cream
* 100-calorie ice cream bars
* Or any brand or flavor that is less than 150 calories per serving

Cookies, Crackers, and Chips

* Nut-Thins almond and rice crackers
* Hard pretzels
* Multigrain crackers
* Baked reduced-fat crackers
* Rice cake snacks (various flavors)
* Brown rice chips
* Kashi TLC cookies
* Organic vanilla animal cookies
* Organic granola bars

Chocolate Lover?

Dark chocolate is better for you than milk chocolate. I know you have heard this before. But why is dark chocolate healthier? Well, for one thing, the level of antioxidants is much higher in dark chocolate than in milk chocolate. Antioxidants help fight off free radicals (cancer- and disease-causing substances) in our bodies. Dark chocolate is also proven to reduce blood pressure and cholesterol levels. So, next time you're stuck between the choice of light or dark, I'd go with the dark.

* No Sugar Added hot chocolate (tastes just as sweet!)
* Dark chocolate (small piece, of course!)
* No Sugar Added chocolate pudding snack cup
* Chocolate-flavored sorbet
* 1 or 2 tablespoons of light or regular chocolate syrup (put over fruit, or mix in with milk)

Well, there you go! You have your very own healthy eating grocery guide. All you gotta do now is get your butt to the store and start restocking your kitchen for weight-loss success! Of course, you don't have to buy *everything* on this list. This is just a guideline. And don't think that if something is not on the list, that automatically means it's not healthy. There are plenty of other foods out there that are OK to eat that aren't included here. As long as those foods meet the same nutritional guidelines as the ones on this list, they're in the clear. Just make sure you check the labels on everything before you buy. If it doesn't check out, back on the shelf!

FOOD DIARY

It's easy to *plan* on eating healthy, but it's also easy to "forget" about your plan. Deciding you're going to start eating healthy tomorrow without knowing what you're even going to eat does not set you up for success. Why? Because with no set meal plan, you'll go for whatever is quick and easy. Usually, quick and easy does not equal healthy. That's why food diaries are so helpful.

A food diary is a place where you keep track of everything you eat and drink. Kind of like your fitness journal, but in this case you're tracking your nutrition. This is how a food diary works: every night, write in your journal (or use an online food journal or food journal app on your phone) what you plan on eating the next day for breakfast, lunch, dinner, and snacks. Here is an example of what a food diary entry might look like:

Monday

Breakfast

Oatmeal, banana,
handful of pecans, 1 cup coffee

Snack

~~Apple~~ + handful mixed nuts
1 orange

Lunch

*+ 3 bites of Mom's fried rice

Mahi, Mahi, mixed vegetables,
1 small potato

Snack

Apple and 1 tblsp. sunflower butter

Dinner

Grilled chicken, salad, 1/2 sweet potato

*bedtime snack - banana, 1 cup hot chocolate

Your goal is to stick to your plan as closely as possible. At the end of the day, go back to your journal and record what you actually ate. Why is a food diary so helpful? Well, most people never pay attention to what and how much they eat. By the end of the day, they don't realize the amount of food they've actually consumed. Until—uh-oh!—they look at the scale the next morning.

This is why it is good to keep a food diary. You're much more likely to eat healthier if you *plan* on eating healthier. A food diary keeps you on track with your diet. You will always know what and how much to eat at each meal. Come snack time after school, when your stomach is literally eating itself, you won't gobble up the first edible morsel you find. You'll already know what you're going to eat and head for that instead.

What you'll learn most from keeping a food diary is portion control. Eat only what you plan on eating, and you'll cut out the extra calories from all your usual unnecessary snacking. And you know what a deficit of calories means, don't you? A deficit of stomach rolls—duh!

Small Changes

Broccoli and carrots and peas—oh my! Yes, healthy food sounds a bit scary to you right now, I know. I mean, who wants to eat mini tree-like plant thingies when you have a freezer stocked with crispy Hot Pockets? Someone who wants to look hot in a bathing suit, that's who! But I do understand that opting for broccoli over your typical vegetable of choice (french fries) is not easy at first. It definitely took me a while to get where I am now. The best way to go about changing your diet is to start small. Here are a few tips to get you going.

Sugary kid's cereal for breakfast? Switch out the Cap'n Crunch for a more grown-up cereal, one that has less sugar and more fiber. Fiber keeps you feeling fuller longer and can also help lower cholesterol and control blood sugar levels. Oatmeal and other whole grain cereals (especially if they are organic) are a better choice because they contain more fiber and usually less sugar. Check out the nutrition labels on the back of your cereal box. If it has less than 3 grams of fiber and more than 5 grams of sugar per serving, it's probably not your best option.

Speaking of cereal . . . What kind of milk are you drinking? If it's whole (4 percent fat) milk, switch to 1 percent or skim milk instead. Or (especially if you're lactose intolerant), choose from the many dairy-free milk substitutes like soy, almond, rice, or coconut milk (my favorite is So Delicious coconut milk—yum!).

Ditch the Wonder Bread. Besides the fact that white bread is filled with HFCS (it's true; check the ingredients!), white bread would still be low on the real food scale. Switch to whole grain bread, which has plenty of fiber, less sugar, and more nutrients that will satisfy your hunger, making you less likely to overeat. Whole grain bread is what white bread was before it was processed and had all of its nutrients bleached out of it.

Drink water, lots of water. Soda, as you may have guessed, is a definite no-no. Water is all the hydration you need and has way fewer calories (0, in fact) than a Coke. Fruit juice is healthier than a soft drink, but you're better off eating the actual fruit. On top of all the naturally occurring sugars, most carton juices have more sugar added to them for a sweeter taste. All that sugar equals calories, which equals fat. Besides, a glass of apple juice won't fill you up. An apple with all its fiber will. Eat calories—don't drink them!

Drink before you eat. Always down one or two glasses of water before you start to eat. Water will make you feel fuller. If you curb your appetite a bit, you won't feel the need to stuff yourself like a ravenous hamster!

Stop mindless snacking. A small snack in between meals is fine, but snacking four, five, six times a day is not. Sure, it may not seem like a few chips here and there or a couple candy bars are all that bad, but they are. Those calories add up! Stick to only *one healthy* snack between meals.

Keep away from the Junk Food Monster! The more you think about food, the more you'll want it. So stay as far away from unhealthy foods as you can. For example, if your parents bring home Burger King for dinner one night, make your own *healthy* dinner and eat it in another room. Don't even enter the dining room until your family is done eating. If your parents have a problem with this, explain to them why it is important for you to not be around unhealthy food. Tell them that you appreciate the fact that they bought you a meal, but Whoppers and french fries are not supportive of your health goals right now.

Whit's Tip

Don't wait until tomorrow to start eating healthy; do it now! Go into your kitchen and pick out the healthiest options you can find. Group them together in the fridge or pantry if you want, or start preparing a healthy meal you can eat for dinner later (remember—the more you plan the more likely you will stick to your fitness goals!). Every meal is a chance to eat better and get closer to your goal. Don't waste any more time!

Homemade simple. How many times do you eat out in a week? Two, three, four, five? Stop! Fast food and chain restaurants add so much fat and sugar to their entrées that you can never be sure what you're really getting. The same goes for your lunch at school. This means stay away from the chicken nuggets and mac 'n' cheese line. Eat your meals at home and start packing your own lunch. This way you won't be stuck eating your cafeteria's daily special (instant mashed potatoes and half-frozen meat loaf—yuck!).

Butter your toast every morning? Not anymore, you don't! There is nothing good to say about butter because it is pure fat. Think about that. What you are putting on your bread is pure, unhealthy fat! Instead, try healthier alternatives to butter like coconut butter, avocado spread, or jam (look for reduced-sugar varieties). These butter substitutes contain fewer calories and have way less saturated fat (remember that's the bad fat!) than regular butter. Another healthy option is to use a little bit of almond butter or peanut butter.

Easy on the oils. While some oils, like olive oil, are good for you, too much of a good thing is just too much. Oils have a lot of calories and cooking with them only adds those extra calories to your food. Be aware of ordering foods from restaurants that are cooked in heavy oils (such as stir-fry and fried foods) and try to avoid them whenever possible. If you're cooking with oils at home, use them sparingly. Measure out your oil by the teaspoon to be sure how much you are really adding into your meal.

Measure out your portion sizes! I can't say this enough. You need to be aware of what you're really taking in. Always read serving sizes on nutrition labels for packaged foods. Before you dig in, know what a tablespoon of peanut butter or three-quarters of a cup of cereal looks like by using measuring spoons and measuring cups. Use suggested serving sizes as a guide for when you eat other, similar foods. Or use the palm of your hand as a guide. When eating foods like nuts, dried fruits, and lean proteins, try keeping your portions no bigger than the size of your palm. As for fresh fruits and vegetables, don't worry about eating too many of them. It's almost impossible to overeat apples or spinach, so eat up!

I know, I know. All of this looks a bit overwhelming. It's OK, though, to try just following one tip a week. See if you can make one change and stick it out every day for just seven days. Add on another tip the next week or keep working on the first until you become comfortable with the change. Aim to fit all of these tips into your daily life. I promise you will see big changes if you do! Soon they will become second nature and won't be such a challenge anymore.

12

Self-Discipline

Self-discipline . . . requires you to connect today's actions to tomorrow's results.

—*Gary Ryan Blair*

Let's play a little game. I call it the "No" game. Why? Because the object of the game is to see how well you can say "No" throughout the day. OK, sounds pretty lame, but let me explain how to play before you make any major judgments.

Many times during the day, you face evil monsters disguised as different foods. At school they morph into greasy pizza in the cafeteria, luring you in with their mouth-watering aroma. In the hallways they serenade you from their hiding spot in the vending machines, pretending to be your favorite candies. At birthday parties you find them in the bottomless bowl of potato chips and in between layers of fluffy frosted cake. Take a stroll through the food court of the mall and you're bombarded by an entire army of monsters that calls to you from the many food displays. Every single one of the little stinkers cries out, "Eat me! Eat me!"

THE "NO!" GAME

This is where the game becomes challenging—because you are not allowed to give in to them. Nope, your role in this game is to see how many times you can say "No" to their tempting advances. And don't be fooled by the monsters' accomplices. They are those people who encourage you to give in.

Let's practice a bit, shall we? Pretend I'm an accomplice:

"Hey, would you like a slice of cake?"

Now it's your turn. What do you say?

"No!" Or, more politely, "No, thank you."

Good job! See, that wasn't hard, was it? OK, let's try it again.

"Do you want fries with that?"

And you say . . .

"No!"

Excellent. It's getting easier, isn't it? OK, one more time.

"Here, take this last chocolate chip cookie—I don't want it."

You know what to say. Ready?

"No!"

Great! You're starting to like the "No" game, aren't you? Oh, come on, you know you are. By saying "No" you strengthen your self-discipline. Don't you like that feeling of empowerment that comes from taking control of your decisions? You see, no one can make you eat the good stuff or the bad stuff. Those choices are all up to you. True, the little monsters make things harder, but they can't take away your free will.

Remember what I said about *your* life being *your* responsibility? In case you didn't notice, that is pretty much the concept behind self-discipline. It might as well be called *self-decision*, because that is all it is. It's a decision *you* make that moves you closer to or farther away from your goal.

Now, let's return to the game. I think we should try something a little more difficult. This time we'll pretend you're alone. There won't be a witness if you succumb to the monsters. You could easily give in and no one will ever know.

Whit's Tip

Are vending machines, drive-throughs, and food courts too much of a temptation for you? Well, one good thing about fast food is that it isn't free. If you don't have enough money to pay for one of Auntie Anne's buttery, salty pretzels, then you're not getting one! Next time you go somewhere fast food is available, forget your wallet at home. Even if you are tempted to binge at the mall food court, you won't be able to! Problem solved.

Let's say you've just arrived home from school. It's been a long day of boring class work, strict teachers, high school drama, and fearsome battles with those devilish monsters. Now you're starved. After carelessly dumping your backpack in your room, you head straight for the kitchen. Oh look, a box of honey glazed doughnuts! You're mom must have gone to the bakery. Hmm . . . this kind of feels like a trap—surely the monsters set this up. But look how shiny they are! Ooooh, and the sweet aroma!

You begin to salivate. Your stomach growls. You hear strange little voices screaming, "Eat me! Eat me!" They're pretty persuasive too. After all, just one doughnut can't hurt, can it? Besides, you can always work it off later.

The strange little voices get more insistent, and you find yourself drawing closer and closer to the doughnuts. You reach out to pluck one from the box, your hands almost trembling in pre–sugar shock, when suddenly thoughts flood into your head of all the hard work you've done lately. All the after-school workouts, the healthy diet you've been following, and that great feeling of knowing you are on the right track. One doughnut could knock you off track and into a dark, cold ditch. Is that what you want? Think about the calories you burned off the night before when you went through that grueling 15-Minute Boot Camp from chapter 9. Give in now and all of your hard work will be erased, because one doughnut will lead to two, then three . . . who knows when you'll stop. And then you'll feel guilty, miserable, and weak.

Are you really going to let a sugar-coated puffy pastry dipped in hydrogenated fat get the best of you? Are you willing to admit you aren't strong enough to stand up to a sugar-glazed piece of bread? With all you've become lately, all the times you've shown yourself to be a dedicated, strong person, are you now going to allow a sugar and fat confection to control you? Not anymore!

Tune out those monsters and let me hear you say it.

"No!!!!"

Yeah! That's what I'm talking about! Sure, the monsters almost got to you. You wanted to eat that doughnut, but in the end you didn't. And you know why? Because you would rather get stuck in an elevator with that creepy guy from class than stay fat for another year.

Whit's Tip

Your family doesn't have to lead a healthy lifestyle in order to help you live one. If they're willing, enlist your family members as drill sergeants. Ask them to be your diet enforcers. Every time they catch you reaching for a bag of chips, they'll call you out and make you drop it. Hey, if they get really into character, maybe they'll make you run ten laps around the block for every chip ingested. It couldn't hurt!

DISCIPLINE IN THE KITCHEN

See, discipline means staying focused on your goals. You know what you want and you know what you must do to get it. You are in control. It is not the other way around. Food does not have any power over you. Food does not make you pick it up and place it in your mouth. Only your gluttonous little hands can do that.

Of course, as you might have guessed, self-discipline takes time to perfect. You won't make the right choices all the time. It's hard to turn down a milkshake when it's right in front of you, but that doesn't mean you shouldn't try. Passing up your guilty pleasures is difficult, but you have to make the effort. A few failed attempts don't mean you suck at life and should just give up. What it means is you have to try harder.

I'm not kidding about the "No" game. (Well, OK, I'll admit there aren't really monsters in your food, but there might as well be!) I'm very serious. Trust me, this game really does work and no one but you will even know you're playing.

I played the game during the last month of my weight loss, when I was trying to shed the final stubborn 10 pounds. It was summer and there were armies of the little junk food fiends around. My friends and I had sleepovers nearly every night. Meaning every night there were HFCS, food dyes, preservatives, and hydrogenated fats in some form or other. One friend's mom loved having us all over and she loved to make us snacks. At night she would offer kettle-popped popcorn drizzled in warm melted butter and salt. In the morning she would pile our plates with fluffy pancakes drenched in maple syrup. Does that sound disgustingly delicious or what? Popcorn and pancakes are some of my favorite foods! But I had to politely decline her scrumptious offerings. I knew what I was missing out on, but I also knew I wanted to lose those last 10 pounds.

Oh, believe me, though: I thought about having "just one bite," but by this time I had learned the consequences of that "one bite." Every time the going got rough, when I felt like I might crack, I remembered one thing. Being fat sucked. If reaching the goal I'd been working toward for a *whole year* meant giving up fried cake batter covered in sticky sugar, I would do it.

And then there was the enthusiasm of knowing I had only 10 pounds to go. Ten pounds! Then it would all be over. My years of torment and shame because of my size would all be over. I was so close. Nothing in the world would derail me. Not even a Reese's Peanut Butter Cup.

For me to turn down a Reese's Peanut Butter Cup meant I was on a whole new level of self-discipline. Sure, by this point I was no stranger to sacrifices. I had already lost 90 pounds, hadn't I? But this time it felt different, much more intense. Each and every day I wrote down what I was going to eat, and that is what I ate. No exceptions, no excuses. In that way I would know for certain what was going into my body. I wanted to be in complete control over my diet. By the middle of summer, I had lost that last 10 pounds, and those pancakes and Reese's that had seemed so heavenly delicious at the time were the furthest thing from my mind.

Whit's Tip

Thinking of just blowing it tonight at your aunt's dinner party? First think about your goals, your dreams, all the reasons you wanted to lose weight in the first place. Do you remember now why you have been putting so much effort into staying on track? Write these reasons down in your journal, on a piece of paper, or on your phone even. Carry this list with you everywhere you go. Bring out this list whenever you have a moment of weakness. Remind yourself why you do not want to give in. Just say *"No!"*

But didn't I feel deprived? Wasn't I upset I couldn't blimp out on Cheez-Its and Twizzlers like everyone else? Well, let's see. The only thing I was deprived of was 10 pounds of fat and I wasn't that upset to see it go. Actually, the more disciplined I became the better I felt. I remember how happy I was each time I said "No" and kept to my meal plan. There I was, losing pounds and getting closer and closer to my goal, while I watched everyone else gorge themselves with foods that had caused all my problems in the first place. Me? Deprived? Please. Finally becoming an "unfat girl" was not what I would call deprivation. It was such a rush when I realized I was in control and I didn't need junk food to feel good. Food didn't control me any longer. My addiction was cured!

Disciplining yourself will require effort, like everything else worth doing in life. But you can make it easier on yourself. Keep your mind off food as much as possible. You know the cheesecake that sings to you every time you open the fridge? Throw it out! Better yet, don't let it into your house to begin with. And don't buy junk food at all. I realize you may not have control over what finds its way into your pantry. In that case, stay as far away from these bad foods as you can. Don't go into the pantry. Why tempt yourself unnecessarily? When your little brother leaves the package of chocolate chip cookies on the counter, put them back into the pantry. If you don't, you'll find yourself staring them down every time you pass through the kitchen, and their moist, chocolaty goodness will be brought to your attention. Soon your craving for a chocolate chip cookie will overwhelm your taste buds and it will quickly find its way to your thighs.

When you find yourself thinking this much about food, immediately turn your thoughts to something else. The less attention you give that tempting slice of cheesecake, the weaker its appeal becomes. Try anything you can to stop thinking about food. Go for a walk. Read a book. Exercise. Wash your parents' car . . . just kidding. The key is to stay busy. Have you ever noticed that when you are really into doing something or having a lot of fun, the thought of food doesn't even cross your mind? In fact, you often don't realize you're hungry until your stomach growls. You were so focused on whatever you were doing that food was the last thing on your mind. Much of the time we only eat because, well, we're bored. So don't get bored!

DISCIPLINE ON THE TRACK

I was strict with my workout plan too. Nearly every day I ran at least two miles. I made sure to get that run in. Sometimes it wasn't easy because I was tired, stressed, or unmotivated, but I forced myself to do it anyway. And I was always glad I did. Discovering I had this kind of control made my confidence soar. If I could be so disciplined with my diet and exercise and get the results I'd gotten, what would happen if I put that same kind of effort toward something else on my list?

You can control your urges. You can overcome the feeling of laziness that settles over you when you think about exercising. You can do amazing things with even a little bit of discipline and determination. However, you'll never know just what you can do until you try. Challenges make you stronger, and that is exactly what this will be—a challenge.

TEMPTATIONS

Some well-known temptations for those of us trying to kick the good ol' food addiction are restaurants, sleepovers, and holidays. Lucky for you, I have some tips for making it through.

Tips for Eating Well While Eating Out

Be on guard anytime you go out to eat. Just because a restaurant does not serve fast food does not necessarily make the food good for you. Both independent and chain restaurants have sneaky ways of fattening you up and keeping you coming back for more. These quick tips will help you stay on track when you find yourself sitting in a restaurant booth.

Do the math. Before you go out, look up the nutritional information for the restaurant where you will be eating. Sometimes the restaurant will put its menu's nutritional info on its website. If not, websites such as CalorieKing.com post the calorie content of menu items for many chain restaurants. Adding up the calories and grams of fat in that lasagna dish you were planning on ordering might make you think twice about doing so.

Fit Chick Chats

purplegirl3: My name is Alexis and I am 13. I weigh 190 lbs. :(I have been overweight my whole life. My mom is also overweight and everyone in my house eats unhealthy. I am tired of having to squeeze into my jeans and having to wear big shirts that don't squeeze my back fat. I have tried many weight-loss programs since I was about ten (including: hip hop abs, slim in six, and EA sports active). None of them work! I really want to drop at least 40 lbs. I really want to do this for myself because I want to get a cute bathing suit that I actually like and feel good in. And when next year starts (FIRST YEAR OF HIGH SCHOOL!), I don't want to be overweight and it would be nice to have a boyfriend haha! PLEASE HELP ME!!

WH: Hi Alexis! It sounds like you are frustrated, but don't be! The fact that you have been trying different workout programs is great, that means you are serious about changing. What you need to understand is that exercise is only part of the weight-loss equation. Your diet plays a major role in the results of your weight loss. You can workout all you like, but if you are still consuming more calories than you burn, you will not lose a pound. My suggestion is to keep up with one of the workout programs you have been doing and really watch your diet. Portion your meals and stay away from anything fried, sugary, or creamy. Those types of dishes typically have the most calories, which you will need to reduce in order to start losing weight.

Make wiser decisions. The basic rule for eating out is to stay away from anything fried, anything described as creamy or cheesy, and anything sugary. These foods will always have the most calories and fat. So instead of fried chicken, order grilled chicken. Instead of creamy lobster bisque, order a broth-based soup. Instead of cheesecake for dessert, order a fruit salad.

Don't eat the bread. Ask your waiter to not even bring the bread basket to your table. Not only will eating it spoil your appetite; it will also add additional calories to your meal. Remember, unless bread is whole grain, it has almost no nutritional value. It is only more sugar, more carbs, and more calories that you don't need.

Order a soup or salad before your meal. Filling up on a healthy appetizer will make it much easier to not overeat when your main course arrives.

Watch the condiments. A salad ceases to be healthy when it is drenched in blue cheese dressing. Whenever possible, ask your waiter for lighter options. And always ask for your sauces on the side. This way you can control how much you use. Besides, there is no need to drench your salad with dressing. A small amount mixed thoroughly into the salad will provide all the flavor you need. And watch out for things like mayonnaise and ketchup served on sandwiches. Mayonnaise is full of fat and calories and ketchup is loaded with sugar.

Switch sides. Forget fries or onion rings with your meals. These delicious devils come with practically everything on a restaurant menu. Before you have time to think twice, ask your waiter to hold the salty fiends. Substitute something not fried: for instance, a baked potato or steamed mixed vegetables.

Decide how much you will eat. Restaurants give you enough food in one meal to feed two or three people. Yet once the plate, piled high with yummy food, is plunked down in front of you, you'll devour every last morsel. Tell yourself before you're served that you will eat only a third to a half of your meal. When you get your food, divide it up, eat your portion, and box up the rest. When you don't want to take your food home but don't think you can stop yourself from picking at leftovers, pour the rest of your drink over it. That will definitely stop you from eating any more!

Slow down! Your brain needs time to realize when you are full. So give it enough time! Make your meal last by chewing slowly and taking small bites. Inhaling everything in two minutes will only leave you feeling sick and bloated. Give yourself at least ten to fifteen minutes to eat your food.

How to Avoid the Sleepover Binge

You know what it's like at sleepovers with your girlfriends. Chips, popcorn, cookies, and candy galore. This may sound like a good time, but when you are trying to get in the habit of eating healthy, sleepovers can be an utter nightmare. Surrounded by so many treats, you're going to be tempted to try at least *one bite*. Yet we all know *one bite* always turns into half a tub of ice cream and about a gazillion chips.

Eat before you leave home. Show up for a girls' night out starving and you're only kidding yourself if you think you won't indulge. Four slices of pizza will be down your throat in the first ten minutes. Avoid this pig-out moment by eating something before you meet up with your girls. You won't be hungry, so four slices of pizza won't be quite as tempting.

Bring your own snacks. Movie time at a sleepover means it's time to bring out all things sweet and salty. To keep your own mouth busy while your girls scarf their food down, bring your own stash of snacks. Pack some of your favorite fruit, like a bag full of blueberries, apple slices, and grapes. Or find some lower-calorie versions of your favorite snacks, such as flavored rice cakes or plain popcorn (add a bit of grated cheese for a yummier treat!). They're great for when you crave that crunch, but are way better for you than oily movie theater popcorn or Cheetos.

Don't cave in to peer pressure. Sometimes friends might not understand or even support your healthy lifestyle. Whether they are aware of it or not, friends can really push you off track. I used to have friends who would hold food in front of my face while saying things like, "Oh, come on, one bite won't hurt!" or "Why do you care about being healthy anyway?" or "One piece is not going to kill you." Once they even tried to force feed me a cookie! But I held my ground and remembered that while they stuffed themselves with food, I was getting thinner. Think about that next time you watch your friends chow down!

Host your own sleepover. Why leave it up to your friends to start the party when you are perfectly capable of starting it yourself? If you host the party, guess who is in control of the snacks? That's right, you! Whip up some tasty, healthy treats to share with your friends. This will also be a good opportunity for you to introduce them to your new lifestyle. Look up recipes for easy-to-make healthy snacks and show your friends that healthy is fun and delicious. Who knows? Maybe you will convert one of your friends into a health nut as well!

How to Avoid Holiday Bulge

As if eating right wasn't tough on a regular basis, it gets even worse around the holidays. Halloween, Thanksgiving, Christmas, New Year's, Valentine's Day, Easter, Memorial Day, Independence Day, and on and on. Pretty much every holiday is an opportunity to get off track. And not only do you have the actual holiday to worry about, but also all of the parties leading up to the holiday! And that's not even including birthdays. Sure, *you* only have one once a year, but when you have lots of friends and family members, well, that could mean maybe thirty birthday parties to attend. That's like a whole month of eating chips and cake!

If you really took the time to count up the number of parties, holidays, and special occasions where food is the centerpiece, you might begin to understand why last year's jeans are too small for you. But don't worry—you don't have to totally miss out on your favorite treats throughout the year. Just follow a few guidelines and you can eat your cake without eating away all of your hard work.

Be Picky. Pick and choose the occasions on which you will allow yourself to indulge. Don't use every birthday party, wedding, and sleepover as an excuse to pig out on sweets and caloric finger foods. Instead, save those calories for really special days like *your* birthday, for example. The same goes for the holiday season. Wait to eat those Christmas cookies on Christmas Day, not one for every day leading up to Christmas! Saving those calories for only really special times will save you from extra weight gain and give you something to look forward to. Come that special day, that pie you have been waiting for will taste even better than you'd imagined!

Graze. Allowing yourself a treat does not mean inhaling everything in sight! When faced with a buffet table stacked with an assortment of devilishly delicious foods, you're going to want to try them all. But instead of devouring two or three huge servings of everything, make a sample platter. Try small portions of the different foods in order to get just a taste. Take your time to really appreciate the different flavors. When you're done, wait at least twenty minutes before you decide to go back for seconds. Again, aim for small, sample-sized portions. You don't need to totally stuff yourself to enjoy holiday treats.

Prepare ahead of time. You know you're allowed to indulge a little bit on certain days, but how do you turn down cake when it's not *your* birthday or stay away from the candy jar at your friend's *pre*-Halloween bash? The most helpful trick will be to eat *before* you head out to a party. It will be much easier to resist temptation if you are not starving. And to keep your mind and your hands away from the food, always hold on to a healthy beverage. Sipping on a drink will give you something to do while everyone else is eating. Plus, guzzling a calorie-free beverage will help suppress your appetite.

Don't feel guilty. You might feel like the odd one out being the only person not pigging out at a party. You might also feel like you're insulting your host by not accepting his or her offerings. However, there is nothing rude about taking your health seriously. In a situation where somebody is expecting you to eat, go ahead and tell them beforehand about your new dietary guidelines. If your host can accommodate you, that's great! If not, don't feel guilty for not accepting food you do not want to eat.

IT'S UP TO YOU

Everywhere we turn we are ambushed by food advertisements. They blare at us from the TV, movies, billboards, the mall, even school! They are always there to tantalize you, making a healthy lifestyle even harder to stick to. But don't let them get the best of you. Remember: *you* are in control of *you*. Turn the TV off, flip quickly past ads in magazines, and ignore the billboards. None of these sneaky temptations have any power unless *you* give it to them. Master self-discipline and you will be capable of nearly anything, even losing 100 pounds.

13

How to Deal

> Here's what I tell anybody and this is what I believe. The greatest gift we have is the gift of life. We understand that. . . . We're given a body. Now you may not like it, but you can maximize that body the best it can be maximized.
>
> —*Mike Ditka*

Before I write the closing words to this book and leave you to continue on your weight-loss journey without me, there are a few more things you need to know. I experienced a lot of changes, both mentally and physically, during my year of weight loss. A lot of the same things I went through, you will go through too. I never had a mentor to help me out along the way, but I did the best I could and managed to get it mostly right. What I didn't do right, I'm letting you know now so *you* can get it right. I can't promise your weight loss will be totally smooth sailing, but if you take my advice, you'll be better able to handle the storms.

HOW TO DEAL WITH YOUR CHANGING REFLECTION

My long-harbored insecurities with my body didn't just vanish with the first 10, 20, or even 30 pounds. How could I possibly feel confident when I *still* hated looking at my body? It was wonderful knowing I had gone down a few sizes in jeans. But not so wonderful knowing I still had to buy the largest size in my favorite stores. Even after losing a reasonable amount of weight! And sure, I would feel great after pushing through a super tough workout, until I remembered that I was still not bikini-body ready, even with all the hard work I had been putting in.

On bad days I'd look in the mirror and pick over everything that was *still* not right with my body. I'd get to thinking how unfair it was that I had to be working so hard to look good when most kids in my school didn't have to lift a finger to stay thin. But this negative thinking only led to negative consequences. These were the time periods I would partake in vicious cycles of binge eating and skipping workouts, accompanied by terrible feelings of guilt. Then I'd get angry with myself for sabotaging what I'd worked so hard for.

Whit's Tip

Stop the cycle before it begins. Before you partake in a self-sabotaging binge, ask yourself: *do I really want to do this?* Most likely the answer will be no. What logical reason would you have for purposely consuming more than your body needs, resulting in weight gain? Emotions sometimes get the best of us and we end up making rash decisions we later regret. So if you're upset, take a moment to stop and think logically. Once you are calmed down, you are less likely to do something you will later regret doing.

What didn't quite click for me at the time was how all of my negative self-talk was directly linked to my productivity level. The more I beat myself up, the less progress I made and the more miserable I felt. It was only after I shifted my thoughts to more positive thinking that I got anything done. Negative thinking is one of the most harmful ways to derail your success. Focusing on your imperfections does nothing but weaken your motivation and kill your morale.

I know it can be hard to have a positive self-image when the mirror isn't reflecting back what you want to see. But hey—remember that you are a work in progress. What you see in the mirror now is not permanent. It will take time, but eventually that image will change. So stop yelling at your thighs for being so jiggly! They can't understand you anyhow, and it won't make them any less jiggly or make you feel any better.

Whit's Tip

If you don't have anything nice to say, don't say anything at all! Before you begin a series of self-sabotaging slander, stop, think, and reverse. Turn those negative critiques into compliments. Instead of bashing on your butt for being so wide, congratulate yourself for going down another pants size since when you started. And no, your stomach may not be flat just yet, but it's a lot flatter than when you started, right?

Positive thinking helps. Don't believe me? Well then, think of a time when things were going really great in your life. Maybe you were making tons of new friends or getting along great with your family. For whatever reason, really good things just kept happening for you. Do you remember how you were feeling at that time and, more importantly, what you were thinking about on a regular basis? You were probably feeling pretty happy and thinking pretty positively, right?

Now think of a really negative time in your life. How were you feeling and thinking then? My guess is that both your feelings and your thoughts were consumed by negativity. In fact, I bet the more negative your thoughts were, the worse your situation got. That's because negative thoughts lead to negative outcomes. On the contrary, positive thoughts lead to positive outcomes!

So, the next time you are feeling bad about yourself, take a moment to remember what negative thinking will do for your progress. Then immediately stop those negative thoughts and replace them with more positive ones. Visualize the day you will finally have reached your goal. Feel proud of yourself for having worked so hard. One day soon you will get there! But that all depends on how much progress you make, and that depends on you staying positive.

HOW TO DEAL WITH CLOTHES NOT FITTING ANYMORE

It's important to find clothes that fit you just right. If something is too big or too small, it will make you look heavier than you actually are. That's definitely not a confidence booster! Plus, you want to show off your changing body. Hiding it under shapeless, baggy T-shirts or too-tight tube tops is not the most flattering way to do it.

I went through a lot of clothes on the way down. Luckily for me I have a skinnier older sister who was more than willing to give me her hand-me-downs. But even still, I had a few wardrobe issues. During my in-between phase, I was too small to fit into my overweight clothes yet still too big to fit into most of my sister's clothes. When I had the money (my only source of income back then was babysitting), I would buy something that fit me a little better. But for the most part, I made the best of what I had.

Try adding belts to cinch in the waist of pants that are just a little too big. You might also want to wear more dresses and skirts—these are a bit more flattering when cinched than, say, jeans. Pants made out of stretchy material are great too!

If you don't have a smaller sibling or friend, you may not be so lucky to get hand-me-downs for every size on your weight-loss journey. Of course, you could always head to the store and buy more clothing, as needed. But if you're living off your birthday money from six months ago, that might not be affordable. The good news is there are inexpensive ways to refill your wardrobe.

For starters, check out some thrift shops in your area. You're guaranteed to find clothing there for very low prices, and who knows what cool things you might come across? Consignment shops are another option. At a consignment shop you can find clothing and other items at a very low price, and you can also sell your old clothes in exchange for money or store credit. Check online to find the closest thrift and consignment shops near you. Your wallet will thank you later!

You can also save some money if you're good with a sewing machine. Why not put your inner fashion designer skills to work? Turn that now oversized dress from a few months ago into a new skirt or blouse. Or use the material from last year's homecoming dress to make a cool new blazer. Try it out and see what you come up with. Who knows? Maybe a successful career in fashion design is in the works for you!

HOW TO DEAL WITH PEOPLE WHO DON'T UNDERSTAND YOUR NEW LIFESTYLE

Believe it or not, there are some people who can't understand why anyone would actually *want* to eat healthy and exercise. These are the same people who might mock you for eating salads or accuse you of being superficial for wanting to lose weight and change your appearance. These people could be your friends, classmates, or family members. Maybe these people are jealous that you have more discipline than they do to stick to a healthy regimen. Or maybe they simply don't understand how harmful an unhealthy lifestyle can be on your body.

Your family might take your decision to change as rejection when they see you opting out of an opportunity to indulge in family pizza night. They might mock you for "just trying to be different" or accuse you of "thinking you're better than us" because you don't want to lead the same unhealthy lifestyle they do. Friends might give you trouble for different reasons. They might not like that you are choosing to change your body instead of complaining about it along with them (every group of friends knows they do this!). Or they might feel slighted when you skip a hang-out session with them because you'd rather work out. Some friends might go so far as to sabotage your weight loss by applying peer pressure to talk you out of your new healthy ways.

Whatever the case, these people are discouraging and you need to get them off your back! But telling your friends or family to buzz off might not be the best way to go about it if you would still like to maintain a peaceful relationship with them. Your best option would be to bring your unsupportive friends and family members together and calmly explain to them why you are choosing to lead a healthy lifestyle. Remind them that this is your decision and that you do not deserve to be judged for making a change for the better. Explain how their discouragement is harmful to your success and that you would much rather have their support.

If your friends continue to rag on you, then it might be time to hang out with a new crowd. True friends would not knowingly sabotage your success for any reason. This is not always an easy decision. But if it means the difference between you changing your life *forever* or you staying the same *forever*, you must decide whether or not some friendships are worth it. Don't let anyone get in the way of your goals and dreams. There are other people out there who have the same goals as you do, or can at least support your change of lifestyle. Find them!

Family is not so easy to avoid. You can't just decide to switch out your family members—unfortunately! But you can decide how much you want to be around them. If they don't want to support your goals, don't look to them for support. Love and respect them, but acknowledge that you won't agree on everything with them. Don't leave any room in your life for others who will bring you down, no matter who they are.

Whit's Tip

Why not create your own support group? There are a lot of people (girls, guys, kids, and adults) who have the same weight-loss goals as you. If they are taking too long to find you, go find them! Start a walking club or group exercise sessions or a weekly get-together to dish out support and progress tips. Ask around, hand out flyers, or create an online group through social media venues to find those people. You'll gain support and make some friends, and you just might help someone else get started on their own life-changing body transformation.

HOW TO DEAL WITH "LOOSE SKIN" AND STRETCH MARKS

Sometimes after losing a significant amount of weight, you might find you are left with "loose skin." What exactly do I mean by loose skin? Well, when you lose weight, you also lose muscle mass. As your body experiences a calorie deficit (consuming fewer calories than you need to maintain your weight) it uses stored fat as fuel to give you energy. But fat stores are not the only place your body goes for more fuel. Muscle tissue is also broken down and used as energy in times of calorie deficit.

Muscle is what makes your body appear taut and toned. The less muscle you have, well, the looser your skin appears. Basically, you are what some people call "skinny fat." Unfortunately, the less muscle you have to begin with, the looser you may appear after your weight loss. The best way to avoid loose skin is to start building muscle now (see chapter 9, Get Strong). Strength training during and after your weight loss will help maintain and build muscle tone, thereby reducing the appearance of loose skin.

In some cases you might need to do more advanced strength training to reduce loose skin. Working with a personal trainer who is experienced in weight lifting would be your best option. But if you can't afford a personal trainer, you can research information on strength training yourself. There are hundreds of fitness resources available you can learn from. I list some in the resources section of this book. Check your local library or bookstore for more fitness books, magazines, or videos that will have the information you need.

You might have heard of the surgery that gets rid of loose skin. While this is an option, I strongly suggest you work on yourself through intense strength training and healthy diet first. Also, keep in mind that skin can sometimes take a year or more to reshape itself to your new body. Give your body time to adjust before you turn to surgery.

Remember the teens I told you about who were featured on Oprah Winfrey's show with me? I wonder if they all chose surgery before they really gave a go at natural weight loss. Had they become discouraged and impatient, and so underwent a major invasive surgery that they could have avoided if they had only stuck to a healthy diet and a regular workout schedule? Certainly it takes hard work, a positive mind-set, and a lot of patience to achieve weight loss or any successful endeavor. My advice: don't make a serious decision like surgery before you give it your best.

In some cases there might be areas of your body where your skin never fully snaps back into place. Should you turn to surgery then? Well, that is up to you. If you believe it is something that you cannot learn to accept, or if it severely hinders your self-confidence, maybe surgery is a beneficial decision. After all, I believe you must feel comfortable with yourself to have the best life experience. But first ask yourself: *does it really matter?*

So your stomach might not be as tight as society deems attractive and acceptable? Well, so freaking what?! Society can go take a hike. It's your body and yours alone. If you are OK with your body (after you worked your butt off for months and did something most people never get the nerve to even attempt!), that is all that matters. Don't let anyone—friends, family, boyfriends, peers, or society—dictate how *you* should feel about *yourself*.

Another issue you may find yourself dealing with is stretch marks. Stretch marks are the red and white lines that appear on your skin after you lose or gain weight. Whether or not you're prone to these is hereditary, so if it's in your genes (apparently it was in mine!), you may notice them on your body. Unfortunately, there is not a lot you can do to totally avoid stretch marks or to make them disappear completely. There are, however, a couple things you can do to lessen their appearance.

Cocoa butter may help prevent stretch marks before they appear, and certain creams may help reduce the appearance of existing stretch marks. I haven't tried either, so I can't tell you for sure whether or not they work. But why not try it for yourself? Cocoa butter can be found in pretty much any store that carries cosmetics. For best results, apply it daily to areas most commonly affected by stretch marks (stomach and thighs) while you are losing weight. For special creams and lotions made specifically to reduce the appearance of stretch marks, look online or ask around to find out where they are sold in your area.

Exfoliating with a body scrub or scrub brush is also something you could try. I actually have tried this and believe it helps somewhat. I began using an exfoliating body scrub every day for a few months and noticed my stretch marks were less visible. (The trick is to vigorously rub the scrub into your skin.) An exfoliating scrub brush would work as well, whichever you prefer.

But, like I said, stretch marks are very hard to make disappear completely. If creams and scrubs don't work for you, don't worry about stretch marks. A lot of people have them, even movie stars and models! It sometimes can't be avoided and therefore is nothing to feel self-conscious about. Think of your stretch marks as your battle scars. They just serve as a reminder of what you have been through and accomplished. So you have a few marks on your body here and there? So what!

No one has a "perfect" body. Got that? No one! Perfection does not exist. Everyone has a different body type and everyone has something they consider a flaw. The reality is that there are no such things as body flaws. Why? Because the human body is designed to change, adapt, and grow old. Some things like loose skin, wrinkles, and stretch marks are meant to happen because that's how our bodies naturally react. Does it mean they should be considered flaws? Nature doesn't think so and neither should you. Be proud of your body for enduring the battle you fought—stretch marks, loose skin, and all.

Conclusion

Go confidently in the direction of your dreams!
Live the life you've imagined.

—*Henry David Thoreau*

When I was fifteen, I stepped on my bathroom scale and the number 130 stared back at me. That number brought a smile to my face. It was my reward for a year's worth of hard work and persistence. It was August, only a few weeks before the start of school. I would be going into the tenth grade, my second year in high school but my first year as a completely new person. I was finally no longer the "fat girl" and never again would be.

That summer I'd already had a few new experiences in my new body. My cousin and I went on vacation to the beach, where I'd normally be camped out on a beach towel doing my best to hide my fat rolls. But not this time! I didn't have to stay huddled under my big T-shirt, hiding from all the fun. This time I had nothing to hide and didn't worry about being confused with a baby whale.

Another first for me was being approached by boys. The only time boys had ever looked at me before was to gawk at my enormity. Other than that, they never paid me much attention. But that summer they weren't gawking because of my size. I mean, I was looking good! However, it was still a shock when a group of the *hottest* volleyball players I'd ever seen came up to talk to *me*! Was I on a candid camera TV show? Cute boys never even knew I existed before!

But what was even better than cute boys? Uh, cute clothes of course! Back-to-school shopping was for the first time an exciting endeavor. For years I'd longingly gazed at the clothing in fashion magazines and envisioned what I might look like wearing them. Now, well, I could actually *wear* the clothes I saw in magazines! It was the weirdest yet most exciting feeling to reach for a size small instead of an extra large. It didn't feel quite real, yet it was!

My life was literally a dream come true. Pretty much everything had turned out the way I'd always hoped it would. Well, all but one, that is. When I was younger I used to dream that once I became skinny, the kids at school would finally accept me. My classmates (the same ones who made fun of me) would be nice to me and even include me in their games at recess! I would be friends with everyone and everyone would want to be friends with me. And I would never, ever be harassed again.

For the most part, that dream came true. The same previously catty girls from school were now congratulating me on my weight loss; meanwhile the same jerky boys were being much more charming all of a sudden. It was exactly what I'd always hoped would happen except . . . I didn't exactly warm up to them like I thought I would. I was no longer fat; therefore they no longer had an excuse to treat me like dirt. But what I realized then was that they never had any excuse to begin with.

Losing weight changed me on the outside, but it changed me even more so on the inside. I came to understand that I didn't need anyone else's approval to feel good about myself and that I was equally deserving of respect, no matter what the number on the scale said. So why would I want to be friends with people who judged others based on their appearance? Why would I even want to *associate* with people who would deliberately try to make another person feel bad? I couldn't think of any reason, actually, not even one.

Those same girls and boys who used to seem so intimidating before? Yeah, they were about as intimidating as a teddy bear. I didn't care anymore whether or not they wanted to be my friend. I had my own friends now, the same ones I'd met back in the eighth grade. They stuck by me before, during, and after my transformation. Those were the only kind of people I wanted to associate with.

That day I made up my mind to go for that walk, I don't think I realized how far it would take me. Everything about my life has changed since I was fourteen. I'm happy, healthy, confident, and living the life I used to dream about living when I was that shy fat girl in the back of the classroom. Deciding I was fed up with being that girl is why I am who you see today. The healthier I became, the better I felt, and the more my life improved. This is still true for me today.

Nowadays I'm just as—or maybe even more so—into maintaining healthy practices. I never stopped my quest for a healthy lifestyle once I had lost all one hundred pounds. For me, challenging my body physically is exciting and rewarding. I never run out of ways I can improve; there is always a goal for me to work toward. But whether I'm running, boxing, cycling, or trying the latest workout craze, I know that diet is just as important. That's why I stick to a mostly vegetarian diet of fruits, vegetables, lean proteins (only poultry and fish for me), and healthy fats. I may not be perfect all of the time (who is?), but sticking to a regular workout schedule and healthy eating habits has kept those one hundred pounds off for nine years.

And that's why I wrote this book. I want you to become your best version of yourself! It kills me to see young girls unhealthy and unhappy with themselves. I remember being miserable, shy, and self-conscious and it was no fun. You know what I'm talking about. So don't be miserable, shy, and self-conscious anymore! You won't believe how much your life can change until you decide to change it. All you have to do is take the first step. Soon you'll be *living* the life you dream about while sitting in the back of the classroom.

Acknowledgments

The process of writing and publishing a book is hard work, much more so than I had expected, and not just for the author. Quite a few people played important roles in delivering this book into your hands, and I owe them all a heartfelt thank-you. First on my thank-you list is my agent, Jessica Regel, who has been an enthusiastic advocate for my book right from the moment she responded to my query email. You're the best, Jessica! Next, a great big group hug to everyone at Beyond Words. You guys are great! I'd also like to thank James Alvear, a NASM certified personal trainer and owner of Elite Force Fitness in Germantown, MD, and Holli Thompson, a certified natural health professional and holistic health coach who reviewed the dietary and fitness information in this book for me. Last, but most certainly not least, I want to thank my father, Rick Holcombe. Without his teaching, guidance, and willingness to reread my work a million times over, *1 Year, 100 Pounds* would not have been possible.

Resources

Don't worry; the fun doesn't have to end yet! Just because you've finished this book doesn't mean you're finished learning about health and fitness. I've put together a list of some resources you might want to check out to further your fitness education. The more you know, the sooner you will reach your goals!

COOL WEBSITES TO CHECK OUT!

Teen Fitness Connection (www.teenfitnessconnection.org): I stumbled upon this website while researching information for this book. It's a great site for anyone who is really serious about getting into shape (which would be you of course!). It has tons of great tips on eating well and exercise.

Health Status (www.healthstatus.com/calculate/cbc): Want to know how many calories you are burning during your workouts? Check out this site! It is a calorie burn calculator that tells you how many calories you burn for different exercises depending on your stats.

Wise Geek, "What Does 200 Calories Look Like?" (www.wisegeek.com/what-does-200-calories-look-like.htm): This website visually gives you an idea of what 200 calories of some of your favorite foods looks like. You might be surprised at how large or small the amount 200 calories of some foods really is!

CalorieKing (www.calorieking.com): Next time you eat out, visit CalorieKing before you leave home to check out the nutritional info for the place where you're going to eat. Just type in the name of the restaurant or the food you plan on eating and CalorieKing will tell you just what will be going into your body.

SparkPeople (www.sparkpeople.com): I have heard a lot of good things about this weight-loss help program. If you are in need of a support group, try it out!

My Website (www.whitneyholcombe.com): You know I am there to help! Stop by my site if you ever need more motivation or inspiration. You'll also find my blog there. Feel free to drop me a question or suggestion for a new blog post.

REFERENCES

This book contains a lot of numbers when it comes to what's healthy and what's not. Those numbers came from the following resources, and if you're interested in learning more, I recommend visiting the sites and taking a look for yourself:

American Heart Association (www.heart.org)

BMI Calculator (www.bmi-calculator.net)

Livestrong (www.livestrong.com)

Mayo Clinic (www.mayoclinic.com)

Centers for Disease Control (www.cdc.gov)

FitDay (www.fitday.com)

Dr. Oz (www.doctoroz.com)

Institute of Medicine (www.iom.edu)

FITNESS MAGAZINES FOR INSPIRATION

***SELF* magazine** (www.self.com): This is one of the first fitness magazines I began reading when I started losing weight. *SELF* has a lot of great health tips, and the workouts are pretty easy to follow along with when you're a beginner.

Women's Health (www.womenshealthmag.com): I like this magazine because of the amount of information in every issue. You learn not just what is good for your waistline, but what is good for your health in general.

SHAPE (www.shape.com): *SHAPE* is full of great workouts, both in the magazine and on the website. There are tons to choose from so you will never get bored. Plus, they use a lot of great fitness models who really motivate you to work out!

Runner's World (www.runnersworld.com): If you want to become a runner, this is the magazine to read. It tells you pretty much everything you need to know about running.

FitnessRx for Women (www.fitnessrxwomen.com): Many of the workouts described in this magazine are advanced, but in my opinion, it probably has some of the best information and advice of all the fitness magazines.

Seventeen (www.seventeen.com): In the health section of the *Seventeen Magazine* website, you'll find a lot of useful information. There are healthy recipe ideas, workouts, and a fitness blog you might find useful.

WORKOUT VIDEOS

Cathe (www.cathe.com): I love Cathe's workout videos! I used her core max and gym style legs DVDs during and after my weight loss. She has a ton of different workout videos you can do at home in your living room.

The Lotte Berk Method™ (www.lotteberkmethod.net): This is a great workout when you're first starting out because it is low impact. It uses a combination of ballet and Pilates moves that are really effective at toning your muscles.

INSANITY!™ (www.beachbody.com): These workouts are not for the faint of heart. However, they will give you great results! I love INSANITY™ workouts because they are very intense. You might not want to try them until you get in better shape (they are tough!), but they are definitely worth a try if you like challenging workouts.

ADDITIONAL EXERCISE EQUIPMENT

Resistance Bands: These can be found pretty much anywhere exercise equipment is sold. They are lightweight and can be used in place of dumbbells for some exercises. I like them because they are easy to store or carry with you while traveling (so you can work out while on vacation!). Look online for examples of workouts using resistance bands.

Medicine Ball: Basically, medicine balls are rubber balls filled with sand (or something like sand) and can be found wherever exercise equipment is sold. Typically, they are used for various abs exercises, but you can use them in other ways too. They are really great for adding extra resistance to your crunches or for tossing one back and forth with a friend for an arm workout! Search online for more exercises using medicine balls if you decide to buy one.

Pedometer: A pedometer keeps track of how many steps you've taken. Some come with features that even tell you the exact distance you travel and the calories you burn. A pedometer might be worth getting if you need more motivation to move around. Take it with you everywhere and make it your goal to take more steps than the day before. You might also find a pedometer app on your phone! There's an app for everything nowadays, right?